HIDDEN
HISTORY
of
VERMONT

Mark Bushnell

FOREWORD BY TOM SLAYTON

THE
History
PRESS

Published by The History Press
Charleston, SC
www.historypress.net

Front cover: Young workers at the American Woolen Company in Winooski, Vermont, pose during their noon break in this 1909 photograph by Lewis Hine. The girls are *(left to right)* Bernice Bedard, Sadio Finnogan and Tessie McGarth. *Courtesy of Fleming Museum of Art, University of Vermont. Gift of Daniel K. Mayers 1979.15.7.*
Back cover, top: the Green Mountains, including Camel's Hump, as seen from central Vermont. *Author's photo*; *bottom*: statue of Ethan Allen by Vermont sculptor Larkin Mead. *Author's photo*.

First published 2017

Manufactured in the United States

ISBN 9781625859006

Library of Congress Control Number: 2017948484

To Susan and Harrison, who make the present even more interesting than the past.

CONTENTS

CONTENTS

FOREWORD

For a very small, rural state, Vermont has a lot of history, much of it off the beaten path, some of it inordinately strange.

The state has a heroic origin story that began before the American Revolution and a remarkable record of social causes adopted, advanced and forwarded to the rest of the United States. The scope of Vermont's history and the importance of its influence are far out of proportion to its size.

But also running through our past is a strain of oddities, unusual people and good, old-fashioned weirdness that Vermonters have long savored and to some degree enjoyed.

Sometimes, the heroic and the strange are combined in a single legend. For example, consider the story of Alexander Twilight, believed to be the first black college graduate in the United States (Middlebury College, 1823). In 1829, he came to Brownington and, as principal of the Orleans County Grammar School, started an academy—a residential school for young people. He built a large granite building three stories high to house the school and its students. And how did he erect this imposing structure made of hefty granite blocks? The story is that he used an ox to raise and position the blocks, and when the building was complete and the ox's work done, the builders celebrated by roasting and eating the hardworking animal! The academy building stands today in the middle of the pretty little village of Brownington. It is a museum housing the Orleans County Historical Society and is known as the Old Stone House.

Or consider a more famous hero. Just about every Vermonter knows the name of Ethan Allen. But two prominent Vermont historians have said recently that most of his sizable legend is a nineteenth-century creation and vastly overstated. H. Nicholas Muller and John Duffy agree that Allen was the conqueror of Ticonderoga. He was an off-and-on leader of the Green Mountain Boys, a stirring speaker and a prolific writer.

But he was also a relentless self-promoter who inflated the importance of just about everything he did. For example, he failed to mention that Ticonderoga, when he took it over, was a crumbling, half-decrepit fortress manned by a minimal garrison. Like so much else about Ethan Allen, the fall of Ticonderoga was first and foremost a public relations coup. What he was really good at was boasting, a point Mark Bushnell makes in his essay on Allen.

In the nineteenth century, a farmhouse in Chittenden became the site of a startling variety of ghostly appearances, concocted, in all probability, by the Eddy brothers, who lived there. In mid-nineteenth-century Calais, there was Sleeping Lucy, who claimed to have the power to cure people while she was in a self-induced trance. In 1810, the disastrous escape of Long Pond in Glover occurred. The water burst through a bank that local men were digging in, emptied into the Barton River and roared through the Village of Glover, causing havoc. Fortunately, no deaths resulted. The boggy meadow left by the pond's departure is now known as Runaway Pond.

More recently, the eccentric Ripton millionaire Joseph Battell attempted to ban automobiles from his town. And in another part of the state, another wealthy man, Silas Griffith of Danby, moved to upgrade his reputation as a miser and hard-dealing businessman by establishing a permanent fund to provide Christmas gifts for every child in the area. He also built a library for the town. Griffith is remembered somewhat more fondly in our day than he was in his own.

Of course, throughout its long history, Vermont has had more than its share of noble causes and stirring actions. The state was, famously, the first to include in its constitution a ban on slavery, and its heroic participation in the Civil War is also well known. Vermont has consistently been a firm opponent of bigotry and racism, as evidenced today by its first-in-the-nation legislative approval of civil unions and passage of a statute allowing gay marriage.

But what Vermont may be best known for is going its own way, regardless of the drift of the rest of the nation and the world. Because of its rural isolation for much of its history, its farming heritage, its long-standing traditions, its widespread lack of wealth and its consequent distrust of urban schemes and culture, Vermont has until quite recently traveled a different path. It has prided itself on being self-reliant and stubbornly independent, yet protective of its small-town community connections.

Some fifty years ago, Vermont was politically conservative while the rest of the country was New Deal liberal. And now that the rest of the country is drifting conservative, Vermont may be the most liberal state in the union. The state that in 1936 joined Maine in voting for Alf Landon over Franklin D. Roosevelt can now be counted on to cast its whopping three electoral votes for the Democratic presidential candidate, whoever he or she may be.

That hog-on-ice independence has given Vermont a colorful and unusual history. For years, Vermont readers have been relying on Mark Bushnell to unearth our best historical nuggets and tell the stories in an appealing, accessible way. He vividly captures much of the state's distinct past in *Hidden History of Vermont*. Even today, Vermont continues to go its own way, avoiding the beaten path and creating its own unique traditions.

There is undoubtedly more to come.

Tom Slayton
June 2017

ACKNOWLEDGEMENTS

To be a historian is to be constantly in someone's debt. Naturally, the people we are indebted to are often dead. These are the people, either famous or obscure, about whom we write. Not all of them were good people; some were quite awful. But that's not the way historians judge them. They become our subjects because something about their lives was worth studying and passing on. So my gratitude goes first to those in the past who, whether they intended to or not, lived interesting lives.

But equally important as our subjects are the people who wrote stuff down—the diarists, the journalists and even the bureaucrats. These people make history possible. Otherwise historians, who rely on documents, would be left empty-handed.

Historians are also indebted to other historians. It is always easier to unearth an interesting story when others have already done the spadework. I am grateful for all of the many fine historians who have devoted their attention to this state. I'm indebted to far too many to mention here—that's what bibliographies are for—but I would like to highlight a few. One of the earliest and most influential state historians was Abby Hemenway, whose life's work was compiling stories from around the state and publishing them starting in the 1860s in her multivolume series *The Vermont Historical Gazetteer*. Hemenway's work is idiosyncratic in that it is organized more geographically than chronologically. A more recent and more conventionally organized history is *Freedom and Unity: A History of Vermont*, published in 2004, by Michael Sherman, Gene Sessions and P. Jeffrey Potash, who took on the herculean task of writing a thorough, one-volume history of the state. I have found it invaluable in steering my way through Vermont history and understanding the context in which events occurred.

Other historians have done exceptional work illuminating less-studied aspects of the region's past. During her career, Deborah Clifford focused on the history of women's political and social activism in Vermont. And still others have tackled seemingly well-known topics and debunked cherished myths. John Duffy and Nick Muller did this with particular success in their re-examination of Vermont's most famous hero, *Inventing Ethan Allen.*

I also owe profound thanks to the many librarians of whom I have made unreasonable demands. They have always responded with good humor and great insight and steered me to the right book, academic article or journal entry.

For the last fifteen years, I have frequented the Vermont Historical Society's library, located in the renovated Spaulding Graded School, a large, turn-of-the-century, red stone building that sits partway up a hill overlooking downtown Barre. There are several good places to do research in Vermont. The Vermont Historical Society is my first choice, partly because it's closer to my home, but mostly because its collections are extensive and accessible. And it has a couple of fabulous librarians in Paul Carnahan and Marjorie Strong. They are endlessly accommodating and, best of all, remember stuff. I can't tell you how many story topics have grown out of conversations with Paul and Marjorie. This book wouldn't have been the same without them.

Farther afield, the librarians at Special Collections at the University of Vermont's Bailey-Howe Library, particularly Prudence Doherty and Chris Burns, have been extremely obliging.

Librarians, as a rule, are generous and patient. The same can be said of archivists. Bethany Fair and Rachel Muse at the Vermont State Archives went out of their way to help me locate images to help illustrate this book.

During this book project, I've been fortunate to work with the team from The History Press, including Edward Mack, Lia Grabowski, Chad Rhoad and Rick Delaney, who have helped shepherd this book from concept to printed work.

I also had a secret weapon: two family members who are both accomplished writers and insightful editors—my wife, Susan Clark, and niece Mollie Traver. They were kind enough to read this manuscript and brave enough to point out where I might have been less than clear.

Lastly, I am grateful to you, dear reader, for taking a moment out of your busy life to explore the past.

INTRODUCTION

You hold in your hands a travel book. As you can probably tell from the title, this isn't a conventional travel book. This one won't tell you the best places to eat or where to sleep. Instead, this book is intended to help you travel in time.

Like most travel books, this one will take you to fascinating places, but it will also take you to intriguing times. And it will introduce you to some of the most interesting people there. Of course, I'm not talking about literal time travel—that would be far too expensive, and you would risk not finding your way home. This book is a much cheaper and safer way to go.

I'm talking about immersing yourself in a culture that once existed right here and is separated from us only by a matter of time, not distance. At its most thrilling, time travel can give you the exciting, though fleeting, feeling that you are seeing a place exactly as it once was or that you are witnessing events that happened years ago.

The best thing about this sort of travel is that you get to journey to a distant land without having to worry about learning a new language, missing your connecting flight or knowing the currency exchange rate. But make no mistake, this is terra incognita. As British author Leslie Poles Hartley explained, "The past is a foreign country: they do things differently there."

I hope that through *Hidden History of Vermont* you'll feel you've experienced a bit of the past and understood why people viewed the world the way they did and made the decisions, right or wrong, that they did.

We know, thanks to archaeologists, that people have lived in the place we now call Vermont for more than twelve thousand years. If you want to time-travel here with a historian, the terrain you can visit is limited to a handful of centuries, as it is with all of North America. That's because historians rely on the written word to explore the past. Events that happened before things were written down are technically "prehistory," and the study of them is the work of archaeologists and others who examine the physical artifacts and other evidence of the prehistoric to piece together an understanding of the past.

I write from a historical perspective because it allows me to see and highlight the individual people who shaped events. I think that makes for more compelling stories. This approach has definite disadvantages, however. In addition to restricting the period of study to the relatively recent past, history relies on documents that often failed to record the experiences of much of humanity. Since most of the surviving documents were written by white men, they often overlook the lives of women, Native Americans, African Americans and many other marginalized groups. While I've tried to address that imbalance by searching out and including stories about members of these groups, the historical record, and we historians, are far from perfect.

I've organized the sections—the "tours," if you will—thematically. They run the gamut, from stories about animals, to ones about the singular characters who lived in Vermont, to those about scams, shams and peculiar events. Within each section, the essays are organized chronologically. But there is no need to read them in any particular order. Jump in wherever you like, and keep jumping. Or read the book from front to back, if that's more your style. Like any good traveler, follow your curiosity.

Though reading history is a journey to a foreign land, it is not traveling as far as you might think. As William Faulkner wrote, "The past is never dead. It's not even past."

Indeed, the past informs the present. That's our most basic understanding of history, as a chain of events: everything that exists today has some link to previous times. That is especially true with North American history, which goes back only a few hundred years. Compared to the time humans have lived on this planet, that is the briefest of moments.

I think about that sometimes when I am in a place that hasn't changed much, like President Calvin Coolidge's Vermont homestead in Plymouth Notch. I'll look around and feel almost like, darn, if I had just driven a little faster I might have met Coolidge.

It is the slenderest sliver of time that separates us from our past. I hope that by reading this book, you'll join me in experiencing time travel as if you're visiting a foreign land, one that is both strange and familiar and that isn't as far away as we sometimes imagine.

PART I
FUR, FINS AND FEATHERS

1

THE MOUNT HOLLY MAMMOTH
AND CHARLOTTE WHALE

S ometime about twelve thousand years ago, a woolly mammoth on a hillside in Mount Holly, Vermont, breathed its last. The massive creature, which stood as much as eleven feet tall and weighed upward of six tons, might have died for any number of reasons—old age or disease, perhaps. It might even have found itself on the wrong end of a hunter's spear, because, as odd as it is to consider, Vermont's earliest human inhabitants may have encountered woolly mammoths.

However the mammoth died, its body lay undisturbed for millennia until it was uncovered during the fall of 1848 by some undoubtedly astonished railroad workers. These were the first woolly mammoth remains ever found in North America. Their discovery drew the public's interest, but perhaps not as much as you might expect. In the mid-1800s, Americans were more interested in looking forward than back. People were excited about recent innovations like train travel, whose high speed was redefining how people thought about distance.

For those paying attention, however, the mammoth's discovery helped redefine how people understood the distant past. Most people had trouble thinking of history stretching back more than about six thousand years; their interpretation of the Bible's historical timeline was widely accepted at the time. But finds like the mammoth bones suggested a far more ancient past.

"Extraordinary Fossils" was the headline the *Burlington Free Press* chose for a story it ran three weeks after the discovery. (The artifacts had been buried for perhaps a dozen millennia—so what if it took a few weeks for the news

A fossil discovery revealed that woolly mammoths roamed prehistoric Vermont. This is a model depicting a mammoth at the Royal BC Museum in Canada. *Wikimedia Commons*.

to get out?) The paper reported that the fossils were discovered eleven feet below the ground by workers digging out a "muck pit" to clear the way for railroad construction. The area had apparently been marshy since the mammoth died, creating ideal conditions to preserve the remains.

Newspapers reported that the first piece found was a massive fossilized tooth, a molar in fact, weighing more than seven pounds. Several days later, workers unearthed a decaying tusk measuring four feet long and four inches in diameter.

Newspapers treated the discovery as interesting but didn't delve into what it revealed about the past. The *New Hampshire Sentinel* considered the find as just one of the inexplicable things that had been happening in Vermont lately, lumping it together with the story of Phineas Gage, a railroad worker who had recently survived an accident that shot an iron bar through his brain, and a newspaper report of a man who had survived being struck by a lightning bolt that had badly burned his face and set his clothes alight.

If the general public's interest in the fossils soon waned, scientists' curiosity did not. Louis Agassiz, one of the foremost scientists of his day, understood

Famed scientist Louis Agassiz identified fossils discovered in Mount Holly as belonging to a woolly mammoth. *Library of Congress.*

the fossils' significance. Agassiz had just immigrated to the United States from Switzerland to become a professor of zoology and geology at Harvard. After examining the fossils, Agassiz declared at an 1849 scientific convention in Cambridge, Massachusetts, that, based on their appearance, the tusk and tooth had come from a woolly mammoth, not from a mastodon, as some supposed. (Though related, mammoths and mastodons were distinct species. Mammoths were slightly larger and lived on open tundra, as existed in Vermont during its prehistory, whereas mastodons lived in more forested areas. Among their other differences, mammoths had a hump on their upper back and featured curved tusks, while mastodons had no hump and their tusks were straighter.)

The presence of a mammoth in Vermont didn't surprise Agassiz; in fact, it supported his theory of what life was like here at the end of the last ice age. While growing up in Switzerland, he had seen the landscape patterns created by glaciers and believed he saw signs that the same thing had happened in New England.

Scientists today believe Agassiz was right. They theorize that a mile-thick ice sheet once covered Vermont, creating the landforms we see today as it stretched south and, later, as it melted and receded to the north. Mammals started entering Vermont as the ice sheet began to withdraw some fifteen thousand years ago. In addition to now-familiar species like eastern chipmunk, black bear and white-tailed deer, Vermont was also home to elk, timber wolves, caribou, mastodons and woolly mammoths. The state may have also hosted saber-toothed wildcats, giant ground sloth and giant short-faced bear.

Agassiz soon got more evidence to support his theories of how different the region once was. In 1849, railroad workers made another perplexing discovery, this time in Charlotte, when they unearthed the fossilized skeleton of a twelve-foot-long whale, since identified as a beluga. The whale's discovery helped scientists understand that in place of current-day Lake

Champlain, the region once featured a much larger, salty water body. Now known as the Champlain Sea, this water body covered much of the western part of the state. Today, the fossilized bones of the Charlotte Whale are on display at the Perkins Museum of Geology at the University of Vermont.

The fossilized remains of the Mount Holly Woolly Mammoth, which consisted of two tusks, a large molar, some foot bones and a rib, took a more circuitous route to their current homes. The *Boston Evening Transcript* reported on December 26, 1848, that the "tusks and teeth" could be viewed at Henshaw & Son's in that city. Samuel Henshaw, treasurer of the Rutland & Burlington Railroad, apparently used his clout to obtain the fossils, which he displayed at his brokerage in Boston.

Henshaw offered the bones to Agassiz for his museum, but the scientist declined, saying they would constitute the institution's entire holdings, since the museum was still just a concept. The artifacts went instead to another researcher, J.C. Warren, who created the Warren Museum in Boston. In 1906, after Warren's death, financier J.P. Morgan purchased Warren's entire collection in order to obtain an intact mastodon skeleton that was part of it. He donated the complete collection, including the Vermont mammoth fossils, to the American Museum of Natural History in New York City.

A paleontologist at the museum, Vermont native Walter Granger, decided that the proper place for the Mount Holly artifacts was Harvard,

The fossilized whale skeleton unearthed in Charlotte in 1849 now resides at the University of Vermont's Perkins Geology Museum. *Author's photo.*

since they had originally been offered to Agassiz and Harvard had finally created a museum. Since 1920, when the transfer was made, Harvard has held the molar, nine bones of the foot and a rib in its collection.

The fate of the two tusks unearthed in Mount Holly, however, remains somewhat murkier. Assistant Vermont state geologist Zadock Thompson visited the site shortly after the fossils were found. He described two tusks being unearthed, one measuring eighty inches along its outer curve. The other he described as "badly broken," though he didn't provide any dimensions.

Thompson kept the large tusk for the State Cabinet, a collection of Vermont-related artifacts housed in Montpelier. One of the tusks, presumably the larger one, was later given to the University of Vermont. The university displayed it until several years ago, when the tusk was given, along with a cast of the mammoth tooth, as a long-term loan to the Mount Holly Community Historical Museum. But the tusk on display in Mount Holly measures only about four feet along its outer curve. Thompson noted that the larger tusk suffered shrinkage and cracking after being exposed to the air. Perhaps that explains how it lost nearly half its length since its discovery. What became of the "badly broken" tusk Thompson described is not known.

To add to its long and storied history, the mammoth's tusk and molar received another mark of distinction in 2014. The Vermont legislature designated them jointly the "state terrestrial fossil." As a result, the Charlotte Whale, which had been the sole official state fossil, has had to share the limelight of Vermont fossildom. It is now the state *marine* fossil.

2

THE GREAT WOLF HUNT

The wolves of Vermont were probably doomed from the moment Europeans began settling here. Wolves, like Vermont's more celebrated large predator the catamount, probably inhabited the state's forests until the late 1800s, according to wildlife biologists.

Both predators saw their habitats restricted as settlers cut the forests to make room for farms. With their natural prey limited, both species began attacking livestock, which drew a predictable and violent response from farmers, who believed that the only good catamount or wolf was a dead one.

Historians often cite 1881 as the year the last catamount was shot in Vermont. No one knows when the last wolf was killed, but an event in 1803 suggests that the animal's eventual extirpation from the state was inevitable.

The episode was triggered by the most mundane of events: a boy walking home from school. Eleven-year-old Daniel Baldwin attended school about three or four miles from home, so he often boarded at the school. One Saturday night in February, he decided to make the trek along the Dog River to his home, which was near the border between Berlin and Northfield. His experiences that night were described in a newspaper article that reads like a folktale.

Baldwin first sensed danger when he passed the cabin of Seth Johnston, the last homestead before the trail headed into the forest. Johnston, who was working outside, was alarmed to see the boy walking alone.

"Daniel, you must not try to go through the long woods to your old house to-night," Johnston said, "for the varmints will catch you." He was referring

Early settlers in Vermont feared wolves and hunted them aggressively. *National Life Group*.

to wolves. Baldwin said he wasn't afraid of wolves. It was Johnston's wife's turn to be alarmed.

"Now, Seth Johnston, if that boy will go, you must go with him, or the varmints will certainly have him," she said. "They have been prowling in the woods every night for a week."

But Seth Johnston either was afraid of the wolves himself or couldn't be bothered to escort the boy. Instead, he went into his cabin and returned with a firebrand, a burning piece of wood. If Baldwin encountered any wolves, Johnston told him, he should just wave the "sapling club" around "like fury, and run the gauntlet, and I'll warrant they won't dare to touch you."

The image of having to run from a wolf pack frightened the boy, but he bravely walked on with the burning piece of wood. About a half mile into the woods, Baldwin heard the first howl a short distance to his left. A chorus of perhaps a dozen wolves howled in reply. There was no point retreating, he decided. The howls were coming from every direction, so he might as well keep moving forward. Baldwin imagined the wolves closing in a circle around him. He started swinging his firebrand. He walked faster. His walk became a run.

A dark, yowling figure blocked the road ahead. He sensed more wolves behind him and on each side. Swinging his firebrand, Baldwin pelted toward home, yelling as he went. The wolves kept pace, but the hot, bright firebrand kept them at bay.

The newspaper reported, "[T]hus for the next half mile he ran the fearful gauntlet through this terrible troop of infuriated brutes, till, almost dead with fright and exhaustion, he at length reached his old home with a joy and gratitude for his preservation from a terrible death which no words could describe."

The wolves of Irish Hill, where the incident occurred, would be less fortunate.

The account of young Daniel Baldwin's run through the woods wasn't published until sixty-four years later, when Daniel Thompson wrote it down for the *Argus and Patriot* newspaper of Montpelier. Thompson was a successful novelist, so perhaps he invented or embellished some of the details. But the gist of the story rings true given the aftermath of that fateful walk.

Back in 1803, the story of Baldwin's run-in with the wolves spread quickly. Area farmers had been losing sheep to predators, and this incident convinced them that wolves, perhaps in a pack of as many as twenty, were the culprits. Nearby settlers gathered the next Tuesday and formed a small hunting party on Irish Hill. They killed two wolves but sent out word to surrounding towns that a larger expedition would be launched on Saturday.

That day, four hundred to five hundred men gathered outside the home of town clerk Abel Knapp, according to Thompson. The number seems high in proportion to the region's population at the time, but suffice it to say a large group gathered for the hunt.

The settlers had devised a plan: they carefully fanned out into an enormous circle. Once the circle was completed, word was passed down the line for each man to start walking toward the center, where they believed the wolves were located.

"It was seen and announced that there were enclosed several wolves in the [circle], which ran galloping round the centre, as if looking for a chance to escape through the ring, now become a continuous line of men," Thompson wrote. "The frightened animals could find no outlets, and were shot down at every attempt to escape."

Through this method, two wolves (and a couple of foxes) were killed, but eventually the circle became dangerously small, given that the men were firing into the center of it. At this point, a skilled local hunter, Thomas Davis, was asked to finish the job. Davis ranged within the circle, tracking the trapped wolves. He killed another five wolves and perhaps eight foxes.

The men set to scalping the wolves to claim the state bounty on the animals. By statute, each adult wolf scalp was worth $20 (roughly $850 today); a whelp's scalp brought half as much.

After the hunt, residents prepared supper for the hunters, but many never got a chance to eat. A keg of rum was opened for the hunters, who had grown hungry and thirsty during the day. They drank freely, the rum hitting their empty stomachs. Many were in no condition to eat when the food was finally ready. Thompson wrote: "It was said Esquire Knapp's hay mow that night lodged a larger number of disabled men than were ever before or since collected in Washington County."

The Great Wolf Hunt of Irish Hill was over. According to Thompson, wolves, for better or worse, have never been known since in that part of Vermont.

3

THE SHEEP CRAZE

The *Middlebury Register* ran an unusual obituary on August 9, 1865. The deceased's name was Gold Drop—an odd name for a person, but not for a sheep.

Gold Drop "probably had a better reputation than any [sheep] that ever lived," the community newspaper informed its readers. "He will be sincerely mourned by all sheep breeders at home and abroad."

His death was news. His priceless reputation certainly was not. For three decades, the economies of Middlebury, the surrounding towns of Addison County and, indeed, farm communities throughout Vermont had rested on the sturdy shoulders of nearly two million sheep, especially famed prime breeding specimens like Gold Drop. In an era when fortune hunters were trekking to California for the gold rush, Vermont sheep farmers were striking it rich at home.

These farmers owed their prosperity to two men, a Vermonter named William Jarvis and a Frenchman named Napoleon Bonaparte. While U.S. consul to Lisbon in the early 1800s, Jarvis developed a fascination with the flocks of sheep he had seen grazing in the plains and mountains of Spain. It was their hardy nature and fine, thick fleeces that drew his interest. The breed was called *marino* in Spanish—or *merino* in English—meaning they came from beyond the sea. Spaniards believed the breed originated in ancient Greece.

Jarvis viewed these creatures, and the high-quality wool they produced, as a possible economic boon for his young country and for himself. But

William Jarvis used his connections as a U.S. diplomat to purchase and import merino sheep to the United States. *From* The Life and Times of Hon. William Jarvis: of Weathersfield, Vermont, *1869*.

the sheep were equally valuable to the Spanish, who banned their export. Anyone caught exporting merinos could be sentenced to work in a mine or on a galley ship for life.

The Spanish king made a few exceptions, sending two hundred to the ruler of Saxony (part of modern-day Germany) and several dozen to the kings of France and England as gifts. Two Americans also managed to make themselves recipients of the king's largesse. In 1802, the U.S. minister to France talked the king out of three sheep, and the U.S. minister to Spain somehow finagled two hundred. But, Jarvis wrote years later, "the value of this useful animal was then not appreciated in the United States."

It soon would be. Five years later, in 1807, President Thomas Jefferson imposed an embargo on trade with England to protest that country's seizure of U.S. merchant ships and sailors. Thus deprived of British woolen goods, Americans realized they needed to create their own woolen industry.

It was at this point that Napoleon, emperor of France, inadvertently lent a hand by doing what he did best: invading another country. When his troops attacked Spain in 1809, the Spanish government found itself in desperate need of money—so desperate that it agreed to sell some of its prized sheep. Actually, it agreed to sell flocks seized from wealthy Spaniards who had sided with the French.

Learning of the available sheep, Jarvis dashed off a letter to his friend George Erving, the U.S. minister to Spain. "I have been informed that it is not now very difficult to obtain merino sheep for exportation," he wrote. "If it is not, I am sure that your patriotism will induce you to use your endeavors to obtain me one hundred, principally rams. The cost and expenses within any reasonable bounds, I should not mind."

Jarvis arranged to have twelve of those sheep shipped to the United States. Months later, he received a letter informing him that the eleven that had survived the journey had been sold for $1,500. It was a bitter disappointment. Perhaps no one else realized how valuable these animals were, Jarvis worried, tossing the letter in a drawer. Only later, when he reviewed the note, did he realize he'd misread it. The sheep had actually sold for $15,000, far more than he had dreamed.

Clearly, some American farmers saw the sheep's potential. In 1809 and 1810, Jarvis bought and shipped 3,600 merinos to ports along the East Coast. He returned to his home in Boston in 1810, sold more than 300 of the sheep and the next spring moved to a two-thousand-acre parcel he had purchased in Weathersfield, Vermont, bringing with him 400 of his best merinos. He employed twenty seasonal workers to tend his large flock, which he bred selectively. Jarvis became a champion of merinos, delivering numerous speeches and publishing articles on the topic.

The timing of the merinos' arrival in America was perfect. The War of 1812 blocked access to the British wool market just when American woolen mills were expanding. After the war, import tariffs supported the domestic market. Wool prices rose 50 percent between 1827 and 1835 even as sheep herds grew.

Vermont experienced a "sheep craze" that changed the state's landscape. Farmers cleared vast parts of the state to make way for sheep pastures, which they fenced in with stone walls. As farmers expanded their flocks to take advantage of this profitable market, they took over for less-successful farmers, who usually moved farther north in Vermont or to the Midwest, where land was cheaper.

"Men counted their flocks by thousands," recalled one Vermont farmer who sold his land and moved. "And as they grew more and more rich in money and sheep, they bought farm after farm adjoining their own and turned them into pasturage."

Not everyone thought it was good that so many farmers were being edged out of the state.

"Beware of the 'western fever,'" warned a writer in the *Vermont Chronicle* of Windsor in 1834, "and above all, sell not your farms to your rich neighbors for sheep pastures."

Few, it seems, heeded the warning. In 1836, Vermont's roughly 285,000 residents shared the state with 1.1 million sheep. By 1840, the sheep population had reached 1.7 million, or nearly 6 sheep for every person. No other state committed itself so strongly to sheep. And no place was more overrun by the creatures than Addison County. Even small towns like Orwell had 22,000 sheep, and Shoreham had 27,000.

As sheep farming expanded, cows became a less common sight on farms. Why put all that time and effort into producing milk, when raising sheep

Highly prized merino sheep sired a sought-after line of offspring. *New York Public Library.*

for wool was so much easier and more lucrative? Farmers, it was said, only needed two shepherds, four dogs and a packhorse or mule to tend one thousand sheep.

But in rushing to embrace easy profits, many Vermont farmers, like investors in the midst of any boom, forgot two important economic tenets: good times don't last forever, and it pays to diversify.

The state's wool industry started unraveling in the early 1840s. Prices dropped as the federal government lowered its protective tariff on wool imports. Only farmers on cheap land out west (including not a few transplanted Vermonters) remained profitable. Vermont sheep farmers just couldn't compete. Some began selling their prized sheep for their meat instead of their fleeces.

The Civil War briefly slowed the slide as Northern textile mills lost access to Southern cotton. But the decline continued after the war. Indeed, between 1840, the industry's peak, and 1870, Vermont farmers thinned their flocks by 64 percent.

But owners of the best-regarded flocks were still able to make money. Now, however, farmers made fortunes by selling breeding privileges, not wool. During the Civil War boomlet, farmers could reportedly earn as much as $25,000 by selling top-of-the-line breeders like Gold Drop, which perhaps explains why he merited his own obituary.

Vermont's merinos had perhaps the best reputation of any in the United States and therefore sold for higher prices. As a result, farmers sometimes shipped sheep from New York into Vermont and then sold them as Vermont sheep. Or, in an even more elaborate scheme, farmers painted them with a mixture of burnt umber, lampblack and linseed oil, a concoction dubbed "Cornwall finish" after the famed sheep-raising community in Addison County. The mixture darkened the fleece and made it slightly greasy, just like the hair of a well-bred Vermont merino.

Buyers duped by the ploy must have eventually suspected they had been had. The lambs they were raising surely had none of the luster of old Gold Drop.

4
Marching Turkeys to Market

If you want something to be thankful for, be glad you weren't a Vermont farmer in the early 1800s. Their work was almost unimaginably grueling. Consider this fact: they would regularly walk their goods to market—in Boston.

The goods they were transporting were animals, and in the fall, that often meant turkeys. Flocks containing hundreds or even thousands of them were destined to end up as the main course for Thanksgiving (a day that was celebrated, though not yet as an official national holiday) or Christmas.

The most amazing thing about the stressful and grueling effort of getting the birds to market alive is that some farmers made the trek repeatedly. They had to; they were that hard up. As impractical as they may sound today, turkey drives were a commonsense solution to a major problem: how to get the surplus of farm-raised turkeys in Vermont to the mass market of Boston. In the days before trains, slaughtering them and shipping them on ice wasn't an option. So, the turkeys had to arrive alive at the market. The only way to get them there en masse was to make them walk.

The number of people going on each farm's excursion may have ranged from several to several dozen, depending on how many birds were available to take to market. The various jobs, however, remained the same. The drovers, as the name suggests, drove the turkeys, using a prod to urge them along. Sometimes, they would sprinkle feed on the ground to coax the birds forward. The drovers occasionally tied a bell around the neck of a dominant turkey, making the others more likely to follow.

In the days before refrigeration, some Vermont farmers walked their turkey flocks to markets as far away as Boston. *Wikimedia Commons.*

Other workers would take up the rear, watching for strays (turkeys had a tendency to wander off and join a different flock when they passed another turkey farm). Workers also watched for predators that might view the flock as an easy meal and even for people who might claim a stray turkey as their own. The drovers relied on others to drive a supply wagon that carried their food and tents, as well as enough corn to help the birds maintain their weight during the trip.

Where each day would end was largely up to the birds. The whole contingent hit the road as early as it could and then walked until nightfall. As dark approached, one of the lead birds would flap its way into a tree, and that was it. The day was over. The other birds would immediately find their own places to roost and nod off.

Charles Morrow Wilson wrote of the problems drovers faced in his 1964 novel *The Great Turkey Drive.* Though a work of fiction, Wilson's book was informed by the oral tradition about the drives. He wrote that drovers faced trouble when they tried to cross covered bridges. Apparently, the birds often mistook the bridges' darkness with nightfall and fell asleep partway across, choking off the bridge. The solution that Wilson's drovers found was to carry hundreds of birds, one at a time, across the bridge and into the sunlight. Sometimes, the drovers carried lanterns, Wilson explained, to try to trick the birds into walking a few extra minutes each day.

Turkeys were, in fact, ill-suited physically for the long walks. Farmers found that they had to tar the birds' feet to protect them during the trek. The awkward caravan could make about ten or twelve miles a day across fields and along the crude roads of the time, so the entire trip could take as long as three weeks.

Often, farmers took the treks on pure speculation. They had no guaranteed buyer at the other end. And if birds died en route—typically about 10 percent were lost to predation, disease and straying—farmers had to do what they could to recoup the loss. Sometimes, they would augment their flock by buying additional birds at farms they passed.

As they arrived in the city, the Vermont farmers fattened up their birds just before selling them. They made their sales and then returned with cash or finished goods that were unavailable in Vermont.

These journeys were undertaken in the fall. At that time of year, the traveling farmers could find leftover grain in the fields for the birds to eat. Of course, it didn't hurt sales that Bostonians were looking for something special to put on their tables for the holidays. An 1830s cookbook notes that Bostonians were sure to find turkeys most plentiful each November and December.

Today, the old turkey drives are remembered in stories and songs. Musical historian Margaret MacArthur helped a group of fifth graders from Newbury, Vermont, learn about their local history by composing a song celebrating the drives.

Long ago there was no money
In the town we live in now.
They sent flocks and herds to Boston
Of turkey, geese, sheep and cows
To get turkeys into Boston,
They had to travel far
So farmers spread upon their feet
Heavy coats of tar

Across the Bedell Bridge
A drover boy named Murphy
Drove on foot to Boston
One hundred fifty turkey

Along the Coos turnpike,
many went astray,
'til he sprinkled corn and gathered
many more along the way.

5

Did the Catamount Return?

If he had it to do again, William Ballou might have kept quiet about what happened on March 24, 1934.

But the Congregational minister and Boy Scout leader from Chester could never have guessed what a furor he would stir up. He couldn't know he was placing himself at the center of a controversy that would divide the state into believers and nonbelievers and that he would be both praised as a great outdoorsman and ridiculed as a rube or, worse, a fraud.

The mistake he made was telling a friend. Ballou explained that he'd been leading a troop of Scouts on a hike near Steadman Hill, a 2,300-foot peak in Chester, when they stumbled upon some large animal tracks in fresh snow. Five inches in diameter and catlike, the prints reminded Ballou of mountain lion tracks he'd seen while living in Wyoming.

He thought these paw prints might prove that catamounts, widely believed extirpated from Vermont more than fifty years earlier, were back. Or perhaps they had never left. To support his claim, Ballou and the Scouts made casts of the tracks.

Hearing the story, the friend tipped off the Associated Press, and soon newspapers throughout New England picked up the news. Some treated the story seriously, suggesting that the catamount—the local term for a cougar, mountain lion or panther—might have been forced down from the hills by a recent cold snap. Others assumed Ballou was mistaken. These "wildcat tales," the *Brattleboro Reformer* worried, would only encourage the "wild and wooly ideas people outside the state acquire about Vermont." In attacking

During the 1930s, William Ballou and his Boy Scout troop tried to prove the presence of catamounts in Vermont. *Vermont Historical Society*.

Ballou, the *Bennington Banner* dragged in his profession. "The astonishing thing about the whole affair is that this graft seems to be worked by the clergy," the *Banner* wrote.

Other papers defended Ballou. The *Springfield Reporter* and the *Vermont Journal* in Windsor wrote that the reverend's "integrity is so great, that were he to tell us that he saw a white blackbird, we should be inclined to believe." Editors of the *Rutland Herald*, unwilling to take Ballou at his word or to dismiss him out of hand, offered $100 "for a panther, alive or dead, captured and killed in Vermont during 1934 and not imported for the purposes of the reward." Some papers worried that talk of roaming panthers would scare away tourists, but others joked that, on the contrary, such rumors would attract swarms of people wanting to collect the *Herald*'s reward.

Stinging from the barbs in the editorial pages of the region's papers, Ballou organized a meeting of believers. "Wealth, social position, office and genealogical trees do not count here," he wrote in a newspaper advertisement announcing the event. "Nothing but panther contacts admit you or a friend of yours who is still loyal."

It must have been a strange event, sort of a cross between a church supper and a UFO convention. Here were perfectly ordinary people who wanted to believe something extraordinary. The roughly one hundred people who attended were asked what type of contact they'd had with catamounts. Eleven said they'd seen the cat's tracks, another sixteen had heard its cry and twenty-six claimed a close encounter of the third kind, an actual sighting. Out of the meeting grew one of the most intriguingly named organizations Vermont has known: the Irrepressible and Uncompromising Order of Pantherites.

After the meeting, Pantherites fanned out to prove their case. They loaded guns to hunt catamounts and fired off letters to newspaper editors to do battle with the vocal anti-Pantherite faction. The creation of the Pantherites unleashed pent-up stories about catamounts. Letters detailing wildcat encounters, some notarized to add authenticity, or at least earnestness, poured in to Ballou.

Mrs. George L. Pratt reported hearing a "blood curdling cry" from a catamount. (In the letters, the cries are always "blood curdling.") Blanche Foster of East Wallingford wrote that on the night of April 12, something stole a bird's nest off her porch. The next morning, she found large paw prints in the snow from an animal that had leaped onto her veranda. She said that the "little male bird came back a little later, no mate, no eggs, no nest….Must have been a panther, no dog ever lived would have been as mean as that."

Edna Kiniry of Windsor might take the prize for sheer pluck. She wrote Ballou of her run-in with a cougar while at a cabin near Mount Ascutney. Just that February, Kiniry wrote, she had seen a catamount near the house. The next day, she took the hindquarters of a slaughtered calf and hung it from a tree. Then she loaded two rifles and a revolver and sat watching from her living-room window. At four o'clock that afternoon, the cat came back. She opened her window only slightly for fear of scaring the animal and "aimed as best I could." She squeezed off a shot and evidently hit the catamount. "He gave one stream-line leap, and I got a thrilling view of a magnificent tawny creature, head and body perhaps five feet long, and tail about four feet in length," she wrote.

Kiniry found blood in the snow and began to track the animal, "but at the rate he was traveling when I saw him last he was, no doubt, down to Chester before nightfall."

She concluded the letter by writing: "The meat still hangs in the tree; I still watch at the window, but I fear I have muffed my one opportunity."

She was hardly alone. In the mid-1930s, seemingly every Vermonter was on the lookout for catamounts. Yet, year after year, the *Herald*'s prize

In 1881, Alexander Crowell shot what was believed to be the last catamount in Vermont. *Vermont Historical Society.*

went unclaimed. That didn't dissuade believers, however. Although Panthermania started in the towns around Chester and would fade after a few years, belief in catamounts has lived on, with reported sightings continuing to this day.

Despite the derision they faced, the Pantherites might have been on to something. Perhaps they were just ahead of events. Though Vermont in the 1930s would have been an inhospitable environment for a catamount, the state became more catamount-friendly in the 1950s as farms began to fail and cleared agricultural land started reverting to forest. Wildlife biologists now say that, while Vermont doesn't have a breeding population of mountain lions, it's possible the animals have been occasional visitors to the state.

Ballou's evidence of a catamount in Vermont, a plaster cast of the tracks he found, was never conclusive. The Boston Society of Natural History dismissed his claim, but staff members at the American Museum of Natural History in New York said the prints were, indeed, from a mountain lion.

Ballou was always sure of what he'd found and was hurt that many people didn't trust his judgment. In the midst of the controversy, he wrote the *Rutland Herald*, "I would just as soon have it broadcast through

New England that I was a fool as to have it intimated that I did not know the difference between a panther's track and a bob-cat's. A person who can't tell the difference between 2½ and 5 inches ought to be put in an asylum."

The Reverend Ballou may have started a craze, but he wasn't crazy.

PART II

SINGULAR CHARACTERS AND SURPRISING EVENTS

6

WILDERNESS, MASSACRE AND CANNIBALISM

Misery stalked Robert Rogers and his Rangers just as they stalked their enemies during the French and Indian Wars.

Racing home through the wilds of Vermont in 1759 after decimating an Abenaki village in Quebec, Rogers and his men nervously eyed the surrounding woods for the French troops and Abenaki warriors they knew must be following. More than fear of attack gnawed at them, however. As they fled, hunger also hounded them. When the corn they had stolen from the village of St. Francis ran out, they ate leaves and mushrooms. When foraged food didn't satisfy their hunger, they cooked and ate their leather straps and cartridge boxes and devoured tallow candles. Finally, they ate each other.

In the years that followed, the Rangers spoke surprisingly freely of the incidents of cannibalism. Perhaps they believed that, given the extreme conditions they had faced, history would be forgiving. In that, they were right. Most people, if they have heard of Rogers' Rangers at all, know them as indomitable colonial woodsmen with remarkable reconnoitering and survival skills who fought for the British during the French and Indian War of the 1750s and '60s.

But that's the adventure-story version of events. History is always more complicated.

Robert Rogers was a tremendously rugged, brave and skilled pioneer, as were his men. He was also undisciplined. Superiors, impressed with his other abilities, were willing to overlook this trait and make him a major.

Major Robert Rogers led an ill-fated raid on an Abenaki village in St. Francis in southern Quebec. *New York Public Library*.

On September 13, 1759, British general Jeffrey Amherst ordered the Rangers to march north from Fort Crown Point on the New York side of Lake Champlain into southern Quebec. There, they would smash the village of St. Francis, home of Abenaki who had sided with the French.

The Rangers packed lightly to move quickly. They planned to pick up supplies at Missisquoi Bay at the north end of Lake Champlain that would sustain them until they reached St. Francis. After the raid, they would seize more food from the village and, augmenting it with animals they were able to shoot along the way, make their return. The first sign of trouble came when Robert Rogers and his roughly 140 men reached Missisquoi Bay. The food stashed there was missing, apparently having been discovered by Indians or the French.

Empty bellies didn't stop the Rangers. They snuck into St. Francis and decimated the village. They shot and stabbed anyone they saw and burned most of the dwellings. In his later account, Rogers said his men killed about two hundred Abenaki and suffered only one death themselves. It was more a massacre than a raid if this account is true, but Rogers would be lionized for it. Some historians question Rogers's version. French authorities and the Abenaki believed closer to thirty people were killed, about twenty of them women and children, and that Rogers's losses were worse than he admitted.

As the dwellings burned, Rogers's men ransacked the village and filled their packs with corn. Rangers with different appetites raided the mission church and made off with gold coins, candlesticks and a large silver statue of Mary. The precious metals took up precious space in their packs and weighed them down. They would be lost and discarded on the journey south, but the items have filled the dreams of treasure hunters ever since.

Now it was time to outrun the French and Abenaki, who Rogers assumed were hunting them. The day after the raid, men were already complaining of hunger. Soon they were asking Rogers to let them split into smaller groups. A group of roughly 140 men tramping through the wilderness wasn't conducive to tracking down game, which the men reported was strangely scarce. Within eight days of the raid, they were completely out of food. Some had had their last meal three or four days earlier.

Finally, Rogers divided his men into eleven groups and sent them along different routes south through Vermont. Three parties were ordered to return to Crown Point. The others would converge along the Connecticut River, which they would follow to Fort No. 4 in Charlestown, New Hampshire.

Since waterways were the highways of the day, the men's escape routes read like a river atlas of Vermont. Some groups took the Clyde River to Island Pond, then the Nulhegan River to the Connecticut. Others found their way along the Barton, Wells and Passumpsic Rivers.

Rogers was right: the French and Abenaki were on their trail. The group of Rangers led by Ensign Elias Avery was the first to be attacked. They were surprised near Lovering Lake, just west of Lake Memphremagog in Quebec near the present-day Vermont border. One ranger was tied to a tree and stabbed repeatedly until he died. Six others were taken captive and marched back to St. Francis. Two would be killed there, but four others would be exchanged months later with the British for French prisoners. Three of Avery's men managed to escape their attackers and find Rogers's detachment.

The group led by Lieutenant William Dunbar was even less fortunate. Several days after the attack on Avery's group, Dunbar and his seventeen men were ambushed in marshes south of Norton Pond in northeastern Vermont. By one account, the French and Indians outnumbered Dunbar's group five to one. Dunbar and seven of his men were killed on the spot, their scalped and mutilated bodies left in the marsh. Another three men were marched back to St. Francis and killed there.

Groups that avoided attack still battled with intense hunger. Men began to act irrationally, then became outright crazed. When one party shot a moose and the injured animal loped into the woods, only three men were strong enough to follow. When they found it, the moose had been beset by a pack of wolves. The men apparently challenged the wolves for the meat and were killed in the process.

Lieutenant George Campbell wrote later that some of his men had "lost their senses; whilst others, who could no longer bear the keen pangs of an empty stomach, attempted to eat their excrements."

After cooking and eating much of the leather they carried or wore and having gone three weeks without a decent meal, Campbell's group stumbled upon some butchered human remains. The troops assumed the bodies were "those of some of their own party," Campbell wrote, probably Dunbar's detachment. "But this was not a season for distinctions. On them, accordingly, they fell like Cannibals, and devoured part of them raw; their impatience being too great to wait the kindling of a fire to dress it by. When they had thus abated their excruciating pangs they before endured, they carefully collected the fragments and carried them off."

Others also resorted to cannibalism. The sole survivor of a detachment that had wandered into New Hampshire's White Mountains stumbled out of them with a bloodstained pack and a chunk of human flesh, all that remained of the supply that had kept him alive.

Of the 140 or so men who set out from Crown Point, roughly 50 were dead. The French and Indians had killed 19; the others died on the trek home.

Looking back decades later, one ranger, Sergeant David Evans, remembered not the glory that has been passed down in history books and novels, but a horrific ordeal.

One night during the trek, Evans told a historian, he had searched another ranger's pack and found in it three human heads. Evans admitted that he had cut off a piece of flesh and had cooked and eaten it.

He told the historian that "he would die with hunger, before he would do the same again." Evans was racked with guilt over what he'd done, saying that "when [the Rangers'] distresses were greatest, they hardly deserved the name of human beings."

7

THE OVERSIZED CONFIDENCE OF ETHAN ALLEN

E than Allen was extremely self-confident, arrogant even. But that character trait, or flaw, depending on your perspective, was key to his greatest success, in that people who believe strongly in their leadership abilities often find others willing to follow. Allen's high self-regard, however, also proved his undoing, causing him to overestimate his own capacities and march blindly to his greatest failures.

The high and low points of Vermont's most famous Revolutionary War hero came in the same year, 1775. The success is the more famous incident. If people know one thing about Allen, it's that he led the capture of Fort Ticonderoga at the outset of the war. A less vain man might have been more cautious and missed the opportunity.

From a military point of view, the taking of Fort Ticonderoga was not especially difficult. The fort's occupants, a detachment of fifty British troops, were unaware that violence had broken out at Lexington and Concord weeks earlier; the commander had ignored orders to keep the fort alert to possible attacks; and a section of the south wall had collapsed and been replaced by a wicker gate.

Despite these advantages, of which Allen was aware at the time, the attack was still perhaps ill advised. That's because in the hours before the attack (which would come at dawn on May 10), Allen and his troops still had no way to cross Lake Champlain. The plan called for ferrying the 230 men from Hand's Cove on the Vermont shore to just north of Fort Ticonderoga on the New York side.

Ethan Allen's statue stands at the U.S. Capitol in Washington. *Author's photo.*

But Allen hadn't made proper arrangements to obtain the vital boats. Men had been dispatched to nearby Panton and to Skenesboro (present-day Whitehall, New York) in search of boats, but when Allen and the troops reached the embarkation point, none was in sight. Midnight came and went. Still no boats. The first boat arrived after 1:30 a.m. A second boat reached the cove soon afterward. Two boats wouldn't be nearly enough to ferry all the men across before sunrise, just three hours away.

Rather than postpone the mission for another day, however, Allen still liked his chances. Before dawn, he managed to get barely one-third of his 230 men across the lake. Allen marched the men quietly from the landing site, under the fort's two dozen cannons (which were unmanned) to the fort's gate, which was guarded by a lone sentry. The soldier pointed his gun point-blank at Allen and pulled the trigger. Click. The gun failed to fire. Luck, not just self-confidence and courage, played a role that day. Once inside, Allen ordered a sentry to take him to the fort's commander. A lieutenant, second in command at Ticonderoga, was still pulling on his clothes when he saw Allen at his door. The officer demanded to know by whose authority Allen was seizing the fort. Allen later wrote that he answered, "In the name of the great Jehovah, and the Continental Congress." Some witnesses reported Allen's actual reply as, "Come out of there, you damned old rat!" Others attribute saltier language to Allen. No one was killed or even seriously injured, on either side, in the attack. It was the most bloodless military operation imaginable.

The success apparently went to Allen's head. He boasted about it to all who would listen. Just because he bragged about it doesn't mean the victory wasn't critical. This, after all, was the colonies' first offensive victory of the revolution. The Continental Congress had called on the colonies to fight only defensively, as they had done at Lexington and Concord, in hopes that full-scale conflict could be avoided. Perhaps Allen foresaw that war was inevitable or, in his impatience for glory, jumped the gun. Either way,

An etching depicts Ethan Allen demanding the surrender of Fort Ticonderoga from a startled British officer. *Vermont Historical Society.*

the victory at Fort Ticonderoga only reinforced his already high regard for his military prowess.

The next step in securing Lake Champlain, a vital corridor between British Canada and the colonies, was to seize the one sizeable British warship on the lake. Command of that mission fell to Benedict Arnold, who had vied unsuccessfully with Allen for leadership of the attack at Ticonderoga. As the only officer present with naval experience, Arnold, who would later betray the Patriot cause, was the obvious choice for this next mission.

The boats stolen from Skenesboro, a Tory stronghold, didn't reach Ticonderoga until May 14, four days after the fort's capture. Arnold used those boats immediately to launch his attack, before word of Ticonderoga's fall could spread. Sailing one hundred miles north, Arnold's force entered the Sorel River, where they found the British sloop lying a mile from St. John's and seized it.

Sailing back south, Arnold encountered a ragged flotilla of almost one hundred men led by Allen, heading north. Arnold learned that, hours after his force had left Ticonderoga, Allen found he couldn't contain himself. He wanted to be part of the battle. So Allen had quickly rallied a force, in his haste forgetting to stock adequate rations, and paddled toward St. John's.

When Allen stepped aboard Arnold's prize ship, he must have felt pangs of jealousy. This glory could have been his. In Arnold's cabin, Allen announced that he would take his tired men and attack the town of St. John's immediately. Arnold tried to dissuade Allen, but it was no use. "100 mad fellows are going to take possession of St. John's," Arnold wrote in his journal after Allen left. "A wild, impractical expensive Scheme. Of no Consequence."

As they neared St. John's, Allen learned from a scout that the British, responding to Arnold's earlier attack, had dispatched two hundred soldiers from Montreal to protect the town. Nearing St. John's in the dark, Allen's exhausted men paddled to a spot downriver from the town, climbed from their boats and promptly fell asleep on the riverbank. Their slumber was interrupted at dawn by the crash of cannons from the opposite shore. The reinforcements had discovered them. Allen's men scrambled into their boats and paddled furiously out of the guns' range. In their panic, they left three men behind. One was captured. Two others had to walk the one hundred miles back south to Ticonderoga.

An ordinary man might have learned his lesson and foresworn rash decisions. Not Ethan Allen. That summer, the Green Mountain Boys were converted into a regiment funded by New York. Allen expected to be elected unit commander. Instead, the men chose the more level-headed Seth Warner. Perhaps the men thought Warner was less likely to get them killed. Allen wasn't elected to any post, though his brothers Ira and Heman were made officers.

To Allen's credit, he still wanted to serve during the upcoming invasion of Canada. After friends lobbied for him, Allen was appointed a civilian scout, a position at which he proved quite adept. Allen moved freely and fearlessly behind enemy lines, rallying support among French Canadians and Indians against the British. "I...have two hundred and fifty Canadians under arms; as I march, they gather fast," Allen reported in a note to invasion commander General Richard Montgomery. He said he could raise one or two thousand men, given a week's time.

Allen sent most of his 250 men to Montgomery but still had nearly 100 with him when he hatched a plan. The idea, he later claimed, came from an officer, Major John Brown, who supposedly had raised 200 recruits of his own. They would use their combined forces to capture Montreal. Never mind that neither man had authority to launch such an attack or that

Montgomery viewed St. John's as the more militarily important target. Allen wanted this prize.

Brown's force would approach Montreal from the south while Allen's advanced from the north. When they were in place, they planned to exchange shouts before launching simultaneous assaults. It's still unclear how they thought they would hear each other across what was then a city of roughly nine thousand people.

Allen managed with some difficulty to get his force across a river to the north end of the island of Montreal. There he waited for Brown's signal. It never came. Brown had inexplicably never moved into position. When dawn broke, Allen had no chance to retreat. His force would have been an easy target re-crossing the river. But he didn't move forward, either. Perhaps his confidence finally failed at this crucial moment. Some historians suggest that if he had attacked then, when word of an invading force had spread panic in the streets of Montreal, he might have carried the day.

But Allen waited. Within hours, Quebec governor Guy Carleton rallied troops who descended on Allen and his men. Most fled. Allen and thirty-eight others were captured that day. He would spend the next two and a half years as a prisoner of war. Allen later wrote of the day he was captured, "I thought to have enrolled my name in the list of illustrious American heroes, but was nipped in the bud." As a commander, Allen's impetuousness proved a double-edge sword: it ended his military career prematurely but, earlier, had won him a victory at Ticonderoga that, like Allen himself, is still remembered today.

8

WAS VERMONT EVER A REPUBLIC?

T he coins are a curious reminder of Vermont's past. Minted in the 1780s, they are copper and on one side bear the words *Vermontensium Res Publica*. To some, those words conjure images of Vermont before it joined the Union, when it was a republic—that is to say, an independent nation.

In recent decades, the notion of a Vermont republic has gained political currency. Some Vermonters have argued that the state is no longer well served by remaining part of the United States. Instead, they say, the state should declare itself independent, much as it did in 1777, when Vermont began its fourteen-year run as an autonomous republic.

Of course, the creation of the so-called Second Vermont Republic faces sizable political and economic challenges. It may face historical ones, as well. You can't create a second republic if the first never existed.

The existence of the Vermont Republic is part of popular lore. Many Vermonters trace the state's maverick ways back to the days when it was a sovereign nation. To them, even suggesting that such an entity, or republic, might never have existed is heresy. But some historians do make that claim.

At first blush, it seems odd that there is a debate at all. How can we not know for certain what Vermont *was* between the time it declared independence and when it joined the Union? It wasn't that long ago—we aren't trying to prove the existence of King Arthur's roundtable. The answer should be clear: either it was a republic or it wasn't.

But it's not that simple. Let's start with the basic facts that both sides in this debate agree on. The territory that is today Vermont was in political turmoil when the American Revolution erupted. It was known as the New Hampshire Grants, because the governor of that colony had been granting the right to land in the territory to various settlers and speculators. The colonial government of New York, however, also claimed the territory that was to become Vermont. New York won that debate, temporarily, in 1764, when the British Privy Council set the New York colony's northeastern border at the Connecticut River.

Ethan Allen, his brother Ira and others who owed their land claims to New Hampshire led the most powerful faction in the Grants dispute. When the Revolution broke out, they took the opportunity to declare their independence from Great Britain and, at least as importantly, from New York. At a convention in Westminster in January 1777, they announced that "we will at all times hereafter, consider ourselves as a free and independent state, capable of regulating our internal police in all and every respect whatsoever, and that the people on said Grants have the sole and exclusive and inherent right of ruling and governing themselves."

They named the territory "New Connecticut," in tribute to the colony from which many of the early settlers came. They soon changed the name to the shorter and more distinctive "Vermont."

What exactly were these first Vermonters creating when they established a government to put their declaration into action?

To Frank Bryan, professor emeritus of political science at the University of Vermont, they were establishing a republic. "What does it have to be to be a republic?" he asks. "By any criteria, that's what we were. We passed laws, we formed towns, we minted our own coins."

That isn't enough to convince Vermont historian Michael Sherman, who agrees that during this era Vermont acted with autonomy, but he then adds, "as did many of the colonies."

Did coins minted after Vermont declared its independence signal that it was then a republic or that it wanted to become the fourteenth state? *Author's photo.*

During most of this period, the thirteen former colonies, which did not include Vermont, had declared themselves states but had not yet ratified a unifying federal constitution. They were bound together only loosely by the Articles of Confederation, which remained in place until the Constitution was finally ratified in 1789. "They are all in limbo," Sherman says. "Though they declare themselves independent from Great Britain, they haven't created anything else yet."

To Sherman, what matters is what Vermonters considered themselves; from the beginning, that was as Americans. "If you look at the laws that are passed [during this period]," he says, "they are signed as the independent state of Vermont. They are looking toward becoming part of the United States. They are not declaring themselves an independent nation."

Bryan agrees that most early Vermonters considered themselves Americans. But he considers that irrelevant. "We created a republic until such times as we joined the Union," he says. "Most of us considered [the republic] a stand-in....That doesn't mean we weren't a republic."

To Bryan, Vermont's admission to the Union didn't retroactively change the type of government in place here between 1777 and 1791. And what would have happened if Vermont had been denied admission by the United States? Vermont would have remained what it had been, independent and answerable to no one—in short, a republic, Bryan says.

Sherman, however, says that Vermont's founders never used the word "republic."

Perhaps part of the disagreement is due to the looseness of language. A "republic" could mean any government in which power rests in the hands of the people or their elected representatives. That is the definition now and, according to the Oxford English Dictionary, that was the definition then.

Even if the word *republic* had appeared in early documents—and scholars only seem to have started referring to the Vermont Republic in the early twentieth century—that might not settle the dispute. What Bryan and Sherman are really debating is whether, between 1777 and 1791, Vermont constituted an independent nation.

And what about the words on those old copper coins? Sherman argues that it is a mistake to translate them as meaning "the Vermont Republic." Literally, the Latin phrase *Res Publica* means "the public thing." The coins' minters were simply declaring that the coins were issued under the authority of Vermont, he says.

Others argue that the words were a statement of the type of political entity that Vermont was.

The inscription on the other side of the coin is less open to debate. It reads *Stella Quarta Decima*, meaning "the Fourteenth Star," which signified Vermonters' expectation of joining the Union as the fourteenth state.

The debate over the Vermont Republic will continue to focus on what Vermont's founders thought they had created. What's the right answer? Perhaps it is just two sides of the same coin.

9

THE POND THAT RAN AWAY

Drive north on Route 16 out of Hardwick into the tiny town of Glover and you will pass through a graceful, slender valley. If you stop to read the roadside marker, you will learn a startling fact. Two centuries earlier, the spot where you are standing was seventy feet under water. Though there is little evidence of it today, this valley once contained Long Pond. That is, until one day in 1810, when a grievous hydro-engineering blunder gave Long Pond a new name: Runaway Pond. That error put this town on the map by almost wiping it off of it.

In the early nineteenth century, water was the greatest force humans had harnessed. People set up factories and mills along rivers and streams to tap that power for production. One of those people was an ambitious man named Aaron Wilson (or Willson; the spelling varies in historical accounts). He moved his family from Keene, New Hampshire, to Glover in 1808 to build a gristmill and a sawmill on the Barton River.

Wilson's dream began to crumble only two years later, when dry weather reduced the river to a thin stream. It was then that Wilson had what must have seemed like a good idea at the time. If Mud Pond, which fed the Barton River, wasn't providing enough water, he'd redirect Long Pond so it flowed into Mud Pond. Then his mills would have plenty of water. He ended up getting more water than he bargained for.

On June 6, 1810, Wilson rounded up sixty men, and they started digging a small canal to coax Long Pond to flow north instead of following its southerly drainage. After a morning's work, the men had dug a ditch about

A misguided effort to redirect water flow caused a disaster and turned Long Pond into Runaway Pond. *Vermont State Archives.*

one hundred feet long, five to six feet wide and four to eight feet deep, depending on which account you read. The men stopped a few feet from the north end of Long Pond and broke for lunch. They should never have picked their tools back up. But they did and started to dig out the last feet of hardpan and the curiously sandy soil they had noticed all morning. The sand had made their work light, but they apparently hadn't thought much more about it.

As the last shovels of dirt were removed, Long Pond became free to flow north, down a steep hill into Mud Pond, down the Barton River and then into Lake Memphremagog. The water rushed into the canal that had been dug, but soon the flow slackened and no more water poured into the ditch. Witnesses—survivors, really—describe a moment of eerie calm. They must have stared at each other, wondering "Where is all the water going?"

They soon got their answer. The water was eating into the soft sand, causing the canal to yawn wider. The earth beneath them began to moan and then roar. Trees fell. Half-acre chunks of land, timber still intact, toppled over the eroding bank.

The men ran for safety. One fell into quicksand up to his neck but saved himself by grabbing onto a tree's roots and pulling himself free. Another was saved by a friend, plucked by his hair from the churning, sandy slurry.

Over the next hour and a half, Long Pond ran away. The pond's two billion gallons shot through what had grown into a two-hundred-foot gap. The flood hit Mud Pond below and took all of that pond's water, too. Picking up boulders and trees as it crashed forward, the flood's leading edge presented a forty-foot wall of water. People downstream in Barton heard the growl and thought it was an earthquake accompanied by thunder. But one witness on a hillside saw what was happening: "The forest from Glover was coming down upon Barton."

Fearing that someone might be in Wilson's mill, a man raced more than five miles through the woods, just ahead of the torrent. Some versions of the story say it was Wilson who saved his wife from the waters. Another version says the man who operated the mill saved his own wife.

But Wayne Alexander, a twentieth-century historian who was probably the leading expert on the incident, believed the runner was a young man named Spencer Chamberlain, a tall, wiry man known for his speed. His heroic run is remembered annually on Glover Day, when the town holds a five-and-a-half-mile road race named after what onlookers allegedly yelled as he ran. It's called the Run, Chamberlain, Run.

The water obliterated the gristmill. It also destroyed two sawmills, a blacksmith's shop and five bridges. The flood carried away a horse and numerous sheep. As it flowed, the flood discarded thousands of trees and boulders covered by mounds of dirt in surrounding fields. When the waters reached Lake Memphremagog about six hours later, they allegedly raised the lake's level a foot and sent panicked fish swimming up its tributaries.

Thanks to luck, or to the fact that Glover was sparsely settled in 1810, or to Chamberlain's speed, no one died in the flood.

The aftermath of Aaron Wilson's little project, however, is still felt in Glover. Homeowners in some parts of town have reportedly had trouble digging foundations. Once they reach a depth of about five feet, they hit a layer of downed cedar trees—evidence of Long Pond's sudden demise.

10

CATCHING CANAL FEVER

Technology has a way of exciting people when it annihilates time and distance. The automobile, the airplane, the Internet—they all get you places, physically or virtually, much faster than you could on your own.

In the early 1800s, the technology that had people fired up was the canal. At first blush, transportation canals might not sound particularly impressive; they have been around for more than two thousand years, and boats don't exactly move at breakneck speeds in canals. But to someone whose world had been limited by the speed of his horse on crude roads or the speed of wind across water, canals were pretty exciting. So exciting, in fact, that Vermonters briefly lost their sense and contracted "canal fever," a frenzy to build canals, even in highly impractical places, like across the Green Mountains.

For people in the hinterlands, the economy was shifting from a subsistence mode, in which people made everything they needed, to one in which they produced raw materials that they could trade for finished goods. Canals, which could connect remote areas with cities, were central to this economic revolution. Vermonters were hardly alone in catching canal fever. The contagion was gripping much of the country. It was touched off in 1825 by the completion of the young country's most ambitious infrastructure project, the 363-mile-long Erie Canal.

By that point, Vermont had already been exposed to the infectious economic benefits of a canal. Two years earlier, the sixty-mile Champlain Canal had opened, connecting the southern end of Lake Champlain to the Hudson River and, therefore, to the large New York City market. The

The Bellows Falls Canal, completed in 1802, was the first canal in the United States. Vermont experienced a canal-building craze two decades later. *Vermont State Archives*.

Champlain Canal wasn't even the first canal in the state. Vermont recorded the charter of a Bellows Falls canal company in 1791. Work was completed in 1802. And a canal on the Connecticut River, in the present-day town of Wilder, started in 1810. These canals bypassed some particularly nasty and unnavigable river stretches.

The Bellows Falls and Champlain Canal projects served as a pair of parentheses bracketing the state, helping to ease the transportation of goods down the margins of Vermont. But what about transporting goods across the state? The cross-state route was slow and arduous at best. To traverse Vermont, one had to travel along primitive roads and by river, with many grueling portages around rapids and falls along the way.

Politicians and businessmen thought they saw a better way. They dreamed of canals connecting both Lake Champlain and Lake Memphremagog with the Connecticut River. The canals were envisioned as part of a water transportation network across a region stretching from Boston to Montreal. Planners didn't seem overly concerned that the Green Mountains stood in the way.

The job of finding a route for the proposed Lake Memphremagog–Connecticut River canal fell to DeWitt Clinton Jr. of the U.S. Army Corps of Engineers. Clinton, whose father had helped push through the Erie Canal, directed a surveying team that plotted three possible paths. The first route they surveyed left Memphremagog by way of the Black River Valley, then passed through Coventry before entering Lake Eligo and moving on to the Lamoille River in Hardwick. From there, it headed to Joe's Pond, into the Passumpsic and Stevens Rivers and then into the Connecticut River. But it was far from a level course. At its highest point, the route rose 1,011 feet above Lake Memphremagog and 1,248 feet above the Connecticut. As part of the route, Clinton suggested boring a two-mile tunnel through a hillside in Walden to avoid the added cost of raising the canal another 128 feet over the hill. Clinton wrote that the tunnel would need to be wide enough "to admit one boat at a time, and with a towing path, and shafts to admit a free circulation of air." The cost of the tunnel alone was an estimated $130,000, a sizable sum in those days. The entire sixty-one-mile route would have required the construction of 350 locks, seven times more than were needed for the much-longer Erie Canal.

The price tag for this route was an estimated $859,000.

Even the easiest route was no simple matter. It would have required running the canal from Lake Memphremagog, past the outskirts of Derby Line (whose residents had evidently lobbied to have the canal run nearby), then down the Clyde and Nulhegan Rivers before reaching the Connecticut. This forty-one-mile water route was hardly flat, either. Its high point was nearly five hundred feet above Lake Memphremagog. The cost estimate was a comparatively cheap $306,000, but that figure didn't include the expensive alterations to the Connecticut River that would have been needed to make certain river sections passable.

Two companies sprang up to argue over how best to tame the Connecticut. Folks with the Connecticut River Company, the "riverites," argued that "improvement" work should be done within the river. Those with the Connecticut River Canal Company, the "canalites," advocated for the construction of canals to bypass the river's wildest spots.

The most ambitious idea involving the Connecticut was probably the proposal to connect the river with Vermont's principal thoroughfare, Lake Champlain. Shallow-draft boats could make it from the lake up much of the Winooski River. From there, engineers hoped to find a route that would link into the White, Waits or Wells Rivers before reaching the Connecticut. Such a canal would be a vital link in the planned canal system between Boston and Montreal. Even if that larger regional network never materialized, supporters argued, a Champlain–Connecticut canal would still have the benefit of easing trade between the two sides of the Green Mountains.

A team of army engineers led by Captain James Graham arrived in Vermont in 1829 to conduct the survey. Graham came away convinced of the canal's importance, calling it "a source of considerable profit to this portion of [the] country." And, despite the challenges that building a canal would present, he wrote that "it is quite practicable to effect a communication by means of a canal between Lake Champlain and the Connecticut River." Graham favored a Wells River valley route.

James Whitelaw, the state's surveyor general, begged to differ. Whitelaw, who had seen huge sections of the state during his career, believed that only the connection with the White River was feasible.

We'll never know who was right. Despite the engineers' confidence that they could build them, the proposed Champlain–Connecticut and Mephremagog–Connecticut canals faced insurmountable obstacles, not the least of which was the ruggedness of the Green Mountains. Rough terrain made the proposed routes expensive and, ultimately, not fundable.

Soon after that, by the 1830s, canal fever abated. People lost their enthusiasm for canals as they saw a new technology on the horizon— railroads—that promised to do a better job of annihilating time and distance.

11

HIKING, BEFORE HIKING WAS A THING

Alden Partridge had an astounding idea: he would hike two of Vermont's highest peaks, Mount Mansfield and Camel's Hump. That might not sound like such a revolutionary notion today. After all, thousands of people hike those mountains each year. But this was 1818, when hiking wasn't exactly a popular sport. Merely saying you wanted to climb a tall mountain may have made you seem eccentric.

The other remarkable thing about Partridge's idea is how he planned to get to and from the mountains. Though this was still three decades before the arrival of railroads, Partridge could have traveled there largely by a combination of horse and boat. Instead, he opted to make the trek—a 150-plus-mile round-trip from his home in Norwich, Vermont—entirely on foot. He completed the journey in a week, mostly in the rain.

During Partridge's lifetime of hikes, however, this trek hardly stands out. Partridge was New England's first long-distance hiker. He wrote widely circulated newspaper columns about his wilderness treks and in so doing helped popularize the sport of hiking. In the history of East Coast hiking, all trails seem to lead back to Partridge. Some writers link his hikes to the tourism boom that hit New Hampshire's White Mountains—and, to a lesser extent, Vermont's Green Mountains and Taconics—in the mid-1800s. In the early 1900s, reports of his exploits inspired schoolteacher James P. Taylor to create the Long Trail, which runs the length of Vermont. The Long Trail, in turn, helped inspire Benton MacKaye's vision for an Appalachian Trail, which now runs from Georgia to Maine.

Alden Partridge, the founder of Norwich University, helped pioneer the sport of long-distance hiking. *Norwich University*.

As heartened as Partridge would be to learn that his love of hiking had proved inspirational, he was pursuing his passion for another purpose; he was trying to craft hardy citizen soldiers and give them what he termed a "physical education" to complement their book learning. Partridge, whose father was a Revolutionary War veteran, was a career army officer. He was born in Norwich, Vermont, and attended nearby Dartmouth College before transferring to West Point, where, after graduating, he taught mathematics and engineering.

In 1814, he was named superintendent of the school. But his tenure was short-lived. His changes to the curriculum and administration of the school proved unpopular with superiors, who dismissed him. Partridge's response showed a stubborn streak—he returned to work as if nothing had changed. His superiors had a different opinion of what Partridge's duty was and decided that he was derelict in fulfilling it. So they court-martialed him; he was cashiered from the army, a form of dishonorable discharge. But President James Monroe interceded, allowing Partridge to resign instead.

Partridge's experience at West Point left him disillusioned about the role of the military in American society. He worried that West Point was creating a professional officer class in control of a standing army, which he saw as a danger to the American republic. Partridge put his faith in local militias run by citizens, so he returned to Norwich and founded the American Literary, Scientific, and Military Academy, a private school to teach young men to become citizen soldiers. It was the first school of its kind in the United States. Partridge would found similar schools in Delaware, Virginia, Pennsylvania and New Hampshire. His Vermont school would become known as Norwich University (though it would move briefly to Connecticut and is now located in Northfield, Vermont).

It was shortly after resigning from the army and while his military academy was still just a dream that Partridge set out on his expedition to Camel's Hump and Mount Mansfield. Trails in the wilderness were essentially nonexistent, so he bushwhacked up Camel's Hump in a driving rain. At the summit, he pulled a barometer from his pack and measured the barometric pressure, using it to estimate the height of the peak. He determined that Camel's Hump was 4,088 feet high, only 5 feet higher than the peak's accepted height today.

It had been a hard day, Partridge noted in his journal that night: "Not a dry thread in my clothes, and somewhat fatigued, having ate nothing nor drunk anything but water during the day." The next day, he walked to Stowe, where he met an old friend. Together, they bushwhacked to the summit of Mansfield the following day. They were back down by 5:00 p.m.—"as usual, drenched with the water which fell from the bushes in passing through the woods," he wrote. Partridge bid his friend adieu and walked to Waterbury, reaching it at 10:00 p.m. In the course of the day, he had hiked thirty-four miles, a rather pedestrian total for him.

This trek had been mostly a solitary experience. At Norwich, he would make group hikes a regular part of the program. In August 1821, he led a group of eight thirteen- and fourteen-year-old cadets from the Norwich school, as well as a number of Dartmouth professors and students, on the more than seventy-five-mile trip to Crawford Notch in the White Mountains. From there, they scaled Mount Washington, where they slept near the summit before returning home. Two months later, he led the entire cadet corps—roughly one hundred students—on a hike to Woodstock, Vermont, and back. The next year, the corps hiked to Montpelier, where the governor watched them drill.

Then, in September 1823, Partridge marched his cadets to Manchester, where twenty local residents joined them in climbing Mount Manchester. Lacking a trail, they chose a steep route. Later, one of the cadets would recall having to hold on to trees or anything that came to hand "to prevent our falling backward." The hike, during which Partridge measured the mountain's height, took place near the fall equinox. Some suggest that this is how Mount Equinox got its name. During this four-day expedition, the cadets hiked more than 150 miles, covering 45 miles on one of the days.

During his life, Partridge climbed many of the highest peaks in New England. He advised others to do likewise: "Walk about 10 miles per day at the rate of 4 MPH; about 3 or 4 times each year shoulder your knapsack and with your barometer, etc, ascend to the summits of our principal mountains

Alden Partridge hiked two of Vermont's highest peaks, Camel's Hump (*shown*) and Mount Mansfield, in one 150-mile trek in 1818. *Author's photo.*

and determine the altitudes, walking from 30 to 80 miles per day, according as you can bear the fatigue," he wrote.

Both Partridge's love of hiking and his endurance only seem to have grown as he aged. In his forty-fifth year, he hiked 152 miles in three days in order to climb Mount Monadnock in New Hampshire and then hiked 220 miles in four days while climbing mountains in western Massachusetts. On another Massachusetts excursion that year, he walked 300 miles round-trip, including 64 miles on the final day.

Guy and Laura Waterman relate a story about Partridge in *Forest and Crag*, their 1989 history of hiking in the Northeast. Partridge was setting out one day from Concord, New Hampshire, heading to Hanover, when a stagecoach driver offered him a ride. He declined, noting that the coachman would have to change horses three or four miles up the road. He'd see him then. By the time the new horses had been harnessed, Partridge had already passed the spot. The stage passed Partridge along the road before making another scheduled stop. When the stagecoach finally reached the hotel in Hanover, the driver spied Partridge sitting on the porch, reading. The story is no doubt apocryphal. Nobody could walk that far that fast. Or could they?

PART III

SCAMS, SHAMS AND STRANGE STORIES

12

"The Spirit Capital of the Universe"

The Eddys were the strangest family ever to live in the town of Chittenden. At least, one would hope so. Unexplained noises and disembodied voices were said to fill their house. The mother said she constantly heard ghosts speaking. Schoolmates branded the children as freaks because strange knocking sounds kept coming from their desks. Eventually, the strange occurrences at the Eddy house earned it the nickname "the spirit capital of the universe."

Zephaniah and Julia Ann MacCombs Eddy arrived in Chittenden in the late 1840s after selling their farm in Weston. Julia Ann soon developed a reputation as a clairvoyant who could predict the future and converse with unseen spirits. People claimed she got the gift from her great-great-grandmother, who had been tried and sentenced to death as a witch in Salem, Massachusetts. (The woman somehow managed to escape and sail back to her native Scotland.)

Zephaniah was apparently a mere mortal and was more than a little disturbed by his wife's behavior. His concern only grew when he realized that he alone in the family lacked purported gifts. His eight children—most notably sons William and Horatio—began showing signs of their mother's abilities. While the other children slept, the boys would supposedly vanish from their beds and appear in other parts of the house. At school, the boys were disruptive. Their desks didn't always make those strange knocking sounds; sometimes, they would levitate. At other times, spirits would tear books or slates from the boys' hands.

William and Horatio Eddy were believed by some to have supernatural powers. *From* People from the Other World, *1875*.

Zephaniah saw still stranger phenomena at home. Phantom friends would play with the boys or help them with chores, but the ghosts would disappear whenever he approached.

The first time Zephaniah saw William in a trance, he couldn't rouse the boy. He resorted to pummeling William. When that failed, he poured hot water down his back and then dropped hot embers into his hands. Only time managed to revive the boy. For years after, William would show people scars he said his father had inflicted trying to wake him.

If Zephaniah initially reacted angrily to being odd man out in a rather odd family, his mood eventually brightened. Spiritualism was gripping the public imagination. People believed that the divide between this world and the next was thin and that some people had the gift to bridge it. Suddenly, Zephaniah stopped viewing his children as a bunch of weird kids and started seeing them as valuable assets. A skeptic would say this was when Zephaniah began manufacturing the backstory that became the myth of the boys' psychic skills and peculiar childhood.

For fifteen years, he toured the two boys throughout the United States and Europe. When Zephaniah died in 1861, he left the boys the farm. Free of their tyrannical father and perhaps weary of traveling, they returned to the Chittenden homestead. But they didn't stop performing. Their shows, staged in a theater constructed in their home, attracted visitors from as far away as California and made the town the center of the psychic world.

Six nights a week, the Eddys demonstrated their supernatural prowess to a paying audience. The show centered on William's "spirit cabinet." William would retire to the cabinet—really a small room on one side of the stage—and conjure spirits. Soon after he entered the cabinet, an array of spirits would emerge from it to take their turn on the stage. It was a strange cast—Indians and Africans, a mother and child, a salty sailor, a young girl and countless others—all supposedly the spirits of the dead.

Henry Steel Olcott, a Civil War veteran and avowed skeptic, read about the shows in a spiritualist publication and decided to investigate. He had a reputation for integrity and had been part of a governmental panel investigating the assassination of President Abraham Lincoln. Olcott visited for five days in 1874, trying unsuccessfully to debunk the Eddys' show, and wrote about his experiences for the *New York Sun*. His dispatches proved so popular that he was soon hired by the *Daily Graphic* newspaper to return with an artist and continue his investigations. During that summer, he wrote twice a week of his efforts to disprove the boys' psychic claims.

Olcott tried to maintain scientific objectivity—he hired a carpenter to search for trapdoors in the cabinet and used hot wax to seal mosquito

THE EDDY HOMESTEAD.

The Eddy homestead in Chittenden made the town important among believers in psychic phenomena. *From* People from the Other World, *1875.*

netting over the only window into the spirit cabinet—but he began to believe what he saw. Or at least what he thought he saw. It must have been hard to know what was going on in that theater, since the room was lit only by a dim kerosene lamp located nearly thirty feet from the stage. Over the course of two and a half months, Olcott counted roughly four hundred different spirits emerging from the cabinet.

The most regular visitor seems to have been Honto, an Indian waif who would dance around the stage, play the piano and even sing. Once, an audience member was permitted to touch Honto and reported that her skin felt cool and clammy. Apparently, these were ghosts of the three-dimensional variety.

Aggressive audience members at séances elsewhere learned the same thing when the spirit moved them to take matters into their own hands and tackle the dancing ghosts. In their arms, they would find they held a live person, often the medium himself or herself. The mediums had a ready explanation for this: the spirits had taken over their bodies.

Other contemporaries of the Eddys were equally skeptical. In his wonderfully named book, *The Bottom Facts Concerning the Science of Spiritualism*, John W. Truesdell explained how he thought the Eddy brothers produced one of their tricks in which spirits were said to play musical instruments that lay on a table behind a curtain.

An audience volunteer would be asked to come to the stage and sit with his hands on his knees in front of the curtain. One of the Eddys and a co-conspirator would sit on either side of the volunteer, each holding one of the volunteer's arms with both hands. A sheet would then be placed over the front of the three, as if they were all getting a haircut together. This was necessary, the audience was told, because the "physical eye [is] antagonistic to spirit-power." Then other volunteers were invited to examine the instruments on the table behind the curtain and to look for hidden accomplices. Finding nothing awry, they would return to their seats.

One of the schemers would then squeeze the volunteer's arm hard, Truesdell surmised, distracting him enough that he didn't notice the schemer letting go with one of his hands. The schemer was then able to reach his free hand through a hole in the rear curtain and play the instruments. If during their search, audience members had pushed the table out of reach, the schemer would use a cane or a "grab-all" (a weighted net) to pull it closer, Truesdell explained. For added effect, the schemer would pull stuffed gloves of various colors from his pocket

Some of the many characters who supposedly visited the Eddy homestead's "spirit cabinet." *From* People from the Other World, *1875.*

and poke them on a rod over the curtain. In the dim light, this gave the audience the impression that ghosts of various races were appearing.

Olcott, however, reported no such trickery. In fact, after his experiences in Chittenden, he helped found the Theosophical Society, which took as its mission the investigation of "unexplained laws of nature and the powers latent in humanity." The society still exists.

Some contemporaries mocked Olcott's conversion. "He sacrificed his common sense and reason on the altar of superstition and credulity," Henry Ridgely Evans wrote in *Cosmopolitan* magazine. "The Eddy Brothers, rough, uncouth farmers, but possessed of a world of vulgar cunning beneath their bucolic exterior, were too much for him." Actors dressed as spirits had entered the cabinet from a large apartment above it, Evans said, without explaining how he learned this.

If we are skeptical of the Eddys' powers but believe Olcott's reports that twenty or thirty distinct ghosts appeared in each show, the whole town must have been in on the secret. And why not? The clairvoyant Eddys brought visitors and jobs to the town. The evidence of this, however, is scant. Perhaps like the spirits they purported to channel, traces of the Eddys' techniques remain. At least one town historian remembered hearing the mother of a friend letting slip that she had once been an "Eddy angel."

13

CHANNELING CHARLES DICKENS

Charles Dickens had writer's block in the worst way. It had been years since he'd laid down his pen while only halfway through writing *The Mystery of Edwin Drood*. In desperation, some say, he turned to an unlikely assistant. The public was stunned to read that the great British writer had picked an obscure print shop foreman from Brattleboro, Vermont, to help complete his work. They asked why Dickens would choose an assistant whose formal education had ended at age thirteen, someone who was not known as much of a reader, much less a writer.

More to the point, they wondered: hadn't Dickens been dead for two years?

But this was the 1870s, and the western world was in the throes of spiritualism, the belief that the dead can communicate with the living. The public was more than willing to take seriously a claim that the spirit of Dickens wanted to finish the work he had died in the midst of writing.

So Thomas P. James's timing couldn't have been better. James, in his thirties at the time, had only recently moved to Brattleboro to take a printing job. He is said to have first experienced spiritualism soon after reaching town. In October 1872, James and some acquaintances attended a séance in the parlor of the Oak Street boardinghouse in which he lived. During the session, witnesses said, spirits demonstrated a strong affinity for James. At one point, they claimed they saw the table "waltz exuberantly about the room" before tipping over into his lap, which in spiritualist circles was a sign of James's supernatural powers.

At a séance the next night, James appeared to enter a trance and then, grabbing a pencil, dashed off a note to another participant signed by that man's dead daughter. James proceeded to write more notes signed by Brattleboro residents who had died before he arrived in town.

Then his hand scrawled out another note. This one was addressed to himself and requested a private meeting. It was signed "Charles Dickens." James later explained that while he was in a trance, the spirit of Dickens had popped the question: would James serve as his medium so that he could finish *Edwin Drood*? James accepted, and at Dickens's suggestion, he began work on the author's favorite night, Christmas Eve.

Over the course of several weeks, James shut himself alone in a room for hours. Seated at a table with pencils and papers in front of him, James waited for the spirit to move him. Sometimes, it would take only one minute to enter a trance; other times, it took thirty. Stormy weather, he said, made the process take longer.

During the sessions, James was sometimes aware of Dickens sitting beside him, with his hand placed thoughtfully against his head as he dictated. The meetings would end with Dickens touching James with a hand "as cold and heavy as the hand of Death."

When James revived, he'd find papers strewn around the floor. He'd have to read the unnumbered pages to determine their order. He said he once found a note addressed to him among the papers. "We are doing finely," it read. "I am more than satisfied with the result of this undertaking. You have no idea how much interest this matter is exciting here among the hosts by which I am surrounded." Those spirits, too, Dickens hoped, "will find so faithful a worker and one so much after their own hearts." Apparently, many did. The Library of Congress has a category devoted entirely to "spirit writings."

In the summer of 1873, word of James's endeavor reached a world still sad that Dickens had never finished *Drood*. Upon hearing of Dickens's death three years earlier, poet Henry Wadsworth Longfellow—who, like many others, had read *Edwin Drood* in magazine installments—said, "I hope his book is finished. It is certainly one of the most beautiful works, if not the most beautiful of all. It would be too sad to think the pen had fallen from his hand and left it incomplete." Presumably, Longfellow didn't mean that other writers should finish it for him.

Dickens's publishers preferred that the work remain unfinished, but by 1873, two other writers were working to complete unauthorized versions of *Drood*. Unlike James, though, neither claimed to have had any help from

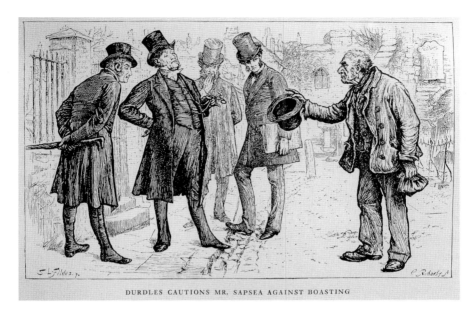

DURDLES CAUTIONS MR. SAPSEA AGAINST BOASTING

An illustration from the 1870 edition of *The Mystery of Edwin Drood. From* The Mystery of Edwin Drood, *1870.*

Dickens. In addition, English theater companies were performing *Drood* plays with their own endings.

On July 26, 1873, the *Springfield Daily Union* in Massachusetts printed long excerpts from the novel that James had completed and said readers would be unable to tell where the living Dickens had left off. The English spelling, the unique diction and other details marked the work as decidedly Dickensian, the paper declared.

The *Union* also added a few stunning details. It hinted that the novel's main character, Edwin Drood, who had been missing and presumed dead when Dickens himself died, had not been murdered. Also, the *Union* reported, Dickens was not through with his medium, whom the paper declined to name. The two would collaborate on a second book, with the bizarre but Dickensian title *The Life and Adventures of Bockley Wickleheap.*

The article in the *Springfield Daily Union* must have thrilled James. In fact, at least one literary historian believes James may have written the article himself. But the press soon turned against James. Just four days later, the *Boston Traveller* printed an article naming James as Dickens's purported medium and attacking his character. James, the paper reported, had led a nomadic life, bouncing among Nashua, New Hampshire; Lowell and Fall

River, Massachusetts; and parts of New York State. Along the way, he had married a much older woman, only to desert her for a younger one. The older woman was said to be suing for divorce, a highly scandalous event in those days. The *Traveller* described James as a "smart, enterprising adventurer, with no nice scruples of honor to embarrass his energies." The paper also reported that James had once told friends he was writing a play. But those who read it said he had merely plagiarized an older play.

Then the *Nashua Telegraph* chimed in. James had worked at the paper three years earlier, the *Telegraph* reported. He'd been a skillful printer but had "a social stain upon his character." James was not educated enough to have perpetrated the *Drood* fraud alone, the paper said; he must have had an accomplice. "Still," the *Telegraph* wrote, "we must give him credit for considerable ingenuity, as the imposition he has attempted is one of the cleverest in conception and execution of modern times. And we shall not be surprised if he attempts with his infinite assurance to bluff it through." The people at the *Telegraph* apparently understood James well.

In October, the book appeared with the title *The Mystery of Edwin Drood—Complete*. The book was credited to "the spirit-pen of Charles Dickens, through a medium." The book also included "that part of the Work which was published prior to the termination of the Author's Earth-Life."

In his "Medium's Preface," James showed that the critics had wounded him. "For some wise purpose, no doubt," he wrote, "the Creator saw fit to place upon the earth a class of people who regard every thing *they* do or say as perfectly right and proper, and every thing other folks do or say as all wrong." Most people, he wrote, understood that an "untoward event in my early life" had no bearing on the validity of the book.

Despite the controversy, or perhaps because of it, the book sold well. James pocketed his profits, left Brattleboro and faded back into obscurity. Whatever James did in his later years, he apparently broke off any collaboration with Dickens, as the world has yet to learn whatever happened to old Bockley Wickleheap.

14

Charity in "The Year without a Summer"

On April 10, 1815, one of the greatest cataclysms in human history occurred, and it was largely overlooked. Mount Tambora, a volcano on the Indonesian island of Sumbawa, exploded in the largest eruption since prehistoric times. Lava flows quickly killed more than ten thousand people on the island. At least eighty thousand more were killed by the diseases, famine and tsunami that followed the eruption.

But Sumbawa was a remote island in the Pacific, and high-speed communication was nonexistent, so word of the catastrophe moved slowly and was quickly forgotten. The impact of the eruption, however, would be widespread and enduring. It was even felt in a corner of Franklin County, Vermont, that would come to be known as Egypt, after the biblical land of plenty, because of a local farmer's response to the disaster.

A year after the eruption and half a world away, Nathaniel Foster, a twenty-nine-year-old veteran of the War of 1812, decided to plant corn in a freshly cleared field. Foster, who was establishing a farm with his new wife, Sarah Leach, hadn't cleared the field entirely; it was still dotted with tree stumps. Like many farmers, Foster had decided that removing the tree stumps was so time consuming and labor intensive that it made more sense to leave them to rot. But rotting was a slow process, so Foster planted his corn among the stumps. Little did he know that the stumps would prove to be just what the Fosters needed to survive the misery to come. Fortunately for many of his neighbors and others farther away, Foster's ingenious mind was paired with a generous heart.

Nothing could have prepared Vermonters for the freakish and devastating year to come. Looking back, people would call 1816 "the year without a summer," "the poverty year," "the famine year" or "eighteen hundred and froze to death." But it started with strangely mild weather. January and February saw high temperatures of forty-six degrees. And March saw a high of fifty-two. That was nothing compared with April, when a heat wave pushed the temperature to eighty-two degrees.

The first sign of trouble came in mid-May. The nights of May 15 through 17 saw hard frosts. Vermonters might have forgotten those frosts by early June, when the temperature rose well into the eighties. But on the night of June 5, the wind shifted and a Canadian cold front drove the temperature down forty to fifty degrees. Two days later, as an anonymous diarist in Brookfield succinctly put it, "Froze all day. Ground covered with snow all day....All the trees on the high land turned black."

Vermont, along with much of the Northern Hemisphere, was experiencing the global cooling effects of Mount Tambora's eruption. The blast had blown an estimated one hundred cubic miles of debris into the atmosphere.

Farmer Nathaniel Foster grew a bumper corn crop in 1816, a time of widespread crop failure. Still, Foster refused to profit from others' misfortune. *Wikimedia Commons*.

One researcher calculated that that was enough dust to cover the island of Manhattan one and a half miles deep.

The high-altitude dust partially blocked the sun, which, to make matters worse, was experiencing a period of particularly low solar activity. In some parts of the Northern Hemisphere, the dust cloud darkened the sky and made it glow oddly. English painter J.M.W. Turner famously captured fantastical skies in paintings like *Chichester Canal* and *The Lake, Petworth: Sunset, Fighting Bucks*, which some art historians now attribute to the amount of ash in the air.

The airborne debris caused global cooling, particularly in New England. Vermonter James Winchester, who was fourteen at the time, remembered the summer of 1816 as the time "when people froze to death in the month of roses—suicides through fear that the sun was cooling off." Without the research and global communication methods that would emerge in the twentieth century, people had little way of knowing that a volcano halfway around the world could be the culprit.

Nathaniel Foster realized that if he did nothing, his crops were doomed. But what could he do? Foster thought of those stumps in the field; maybe they were the answer. He decided to burn them in hopes of keeping the green shoots of his corn crop alive. The stumps didn't burst into flames, but they smoldered. During the worst of the weather, Foster worked day and night lighting and relighting the fires, according to a Fairfield town history.

Vermonters' welfare was linked directly to the harvest, particularly of corn, a staple crop. In those days, most people did some form of farming, whether in large fields or in small yards. Congregations paid their ministers partly in tillable land. Even tradesmen relied on the harvest, as farmers often bartered for their goods.

While people across the state lost their crops, Foster's corn crop thrived, shielded by the warmth from the burning stumps. Not only did he have enough corn for the winter, but he also had more than he could use as seed corn in the year to come. Meanwhile, many other Vermonters feared they wouldn't have seed corn to plant in 1817.

Foster's unexpected bounty could have made him a rich man. The price of corn had skyrocketed. Before 1816, corn generally brought anywhere from $0.75 to $1.12 a bushel in the New York marketplace, according to one study. Because of the early summer frosts, the New York price rose to $1.35 in August and hit $1.78 early in 1817. Prices were dramatically higher in Vermont. In the fall of 1816, a bushel of corn had reached $2.50 in Newbury and $3.00 in Peacham. By spring 1817, a bushel cost $5.00 in Barnard. Some saw the crisis as a chance to get rich. A Newbury man took a boatload of corn up the Connecticut River and sold it for five times the normal rate.

When word of Foster's bounty got out, he received generous offers for his corn. Bankers traveled from St. Albans to visit Foster on his farm and offered him five dollars a bushel. They must have thought they could turn around and sell the corn for still more to desperate Vermonters.

Foster rejected the offer. He wasn't holding out for a higher price; he wanted to sell for less, and not to speculators. Instead, he sold it the next spring to his neighbors and to farmers throughout northwestern Vermont and Canada—anyone who made it to his doorway. The cost? One dollar a bushel. Foster limited how much each person could buy in order to make the seed corn go as far as possible—and perhaps to deter speculators.

People began referring to Foster's corner of Fairfield as Egypt, after the biblical story in which Jacob sends his sons to Egypt to buy corn during a famine.

The story of Nathaniel Foster is largely forgotten today, even in Fairfield. But in the town, you can still find Egypt Road and Egypt Cemetery, where Foster is buried near his lifesaving cornfield.

15

The Varying Accounts
of Sleeping Lucy

Lucy Cooke must have been something of an enigma even in her own day. During her unusual life, Lucy became a healer of local renown who eventually developed a national—some say international—following. What made Lucy stand out was her technique; she is said to have been clairvoyant.

Born Lucy Ainsworth on May 4, 1819, in Calais, Vermont, she was one of nine children. With so many children to raise, the Ainsworths were understandably poor. The older children, including Lucy, were expected to find work to help support the family. Lucy learned to make bonnets and was later apprenticed to a tailor.

Sometime during her childhood, Lucy fell gravely ill. (Historic accounts of her life are vague and sometimes contradictory. In this instance, they don't mention the age at which she became sick. For other events later in her life, they offer little detail of her practice and little substantiation for claims of her great fame.)

What ailed her is unclear. Accounts state merely that she was confined to bed for the better part of two years and that doctors feared for her life. At one point, she fell into a particularly deep sleep. One version of the story says that her brother had returned home from New York State and used his skills at "Mesmerism" to put her into a sort of trance. Mesmerism was named for eighteenth-century German physician Franz Anton Mesmer, who believed in the power of hypnotism to cure patients.

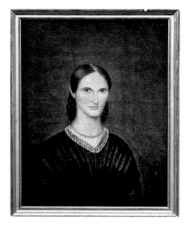

Lucy Cooke became known as "Sleeping Lucy" for treating patients while she was in a sleeplike state. *Vermont Historical Society.*

During her slumber, Lucy later explained, she heard voices telling her she needed to drink a medicine made from certain herbs and roots. As she slept, she supposedly spoke these detailed instructions to those around her. None of the family members had a medical background, nor did anyone know what effect the concoction would have. But given the girl's condition, they apparently believed it couldn't hurt. They prepared the draught according to her instructions, and Lucy drank the medicine. Her health returned rapidly (or gradually, according to another account). From that moment on, according to one version of the story, Lucy began exhibiting extraordinary powers. (Another version says that these gifts didn't emerge until she married at the age of twenty-seven.)

When these powers surfaced, Lucy was reportedly able to dream where people had lost objects. Some accounts suggest she had this skill from early childhood, when in a dream she "saw" where a neighbor had lost his pocket watch. She was even said to have used her mystical powers to help a sheriff with difficult cases.

More importantly, Lucy began to use her talents to cure numerous ailments. Despite her complete lack of medical training, she would enter a hypnotic state and prescribe a cure for her patients. She was even said to set bones and treat dislocated joints with the laying on of hands. When she came out of her trance, she professed no knowledge of what she had done. For her skills and unusual technique, she became popularly known as "Sleeping Lucy."

The times were right for people to entrust their health to a practitioner who relied on a mystical form of medicine. The mid-1800s was an era of extreme change brought on by industrialization, urbanization, national expansion and regional strife. Religious revivals grew up in response to the turmoil. Some people turned to unconventional beliefs; spiritualism captivated the nation with its belief that a parallel spirit world could communicate with and help people in this world. People were understandably impatient with the medical establishment—faced with epidemics and chronic illnesses, it dished out doses of mercury and tinctures of opium.

In 1848, Lucy and her husband, Charles Cooke, moved to Reading, Vermont, and set up practice. Charles is commonly believed to have helped Lucy enter her trances and recorded the prescriptions she made while in that altered state.

Lucy and Charles had a daughter named Julia Ann in 1851, but their family life was short-lived. Charles died in 1855. Lucy and Julia Ann remained in Reading for another five years before moving north to a house on Liberty Street in Montpelier and again starting a practice. An 1860 listing of physicians in Montpelier includes "Lucy A. Cooke, clairvoyant."

After Charles's death, Lucy hired an assistant, Everett Raddin, who presumably took over Charles's role of hypnotizing her and recording her medical advice. Lucy practiced in Montpelier until 1876, then moved to Boston, taking Raddin with her. The pair eventually wed; some of her relatives seemed to believe he did so only for her money. Shortly after this move, Lucy became estranged from her daughter, who was in her early twenties and married. At one point, Lucy is said to have given Julia Ann a dollar and announced that she was disinheriting her.

If her family life was failing, her medical practice was not. In 1878 and 1880, she published leaflets promoting her work. "'SLEEPING LUCY,' formerly of Montpelier, Vt.," read one. "This is the name by which MRS. LUCY A. COOKE has been known to the public for *many years*, and under which she has by her ASTONISHING AND UNEQUALLED GIFTS AND WONDERFUL SUCCESS during that time, acquired a *national reputation* as the *best* and *most reliable* Mesmeric Physician and surgeon of the age."

She challenged the medical establishment but also distanced herself from the charlatans of her era. In her broadside, Lucy challenged any surgeon to best her at setting bones and treating dislocations. She added that "Mrs. COOKE wishes it to be distinctly understood that she is NOT a 'fortune teller,' a 'mind reader,' nor 'a spiritualist.' Her gift is PECULIAR, GENUINE, and WONDERFUL."

The pamphlet claimed that she had "cured diseases of every character" and had treated more than 200,000 people, "many of whom were individuals occupying the highest civil and social positions."

In coming up with that number, Lucy may have included the customers who used her mail-order medicine service. Her leaflets advertised a variety of medicines, each made according to her own recipe. She promised delivery to anywhere in the United States, Canada or the "Old Countries."

For a quarter, she offered Pith of Sassafras, Beth-Root Bitters, Catarrh Snuff and her Cough Lozenges, which the pamphlet said she had supplied for years to "our leading Orators, Clergymen and Singers, for whose use they are the best in the world."

For fifty cents, you could get medicines with such unsettling names as Diuretic Drops, Diarrhoea Cordial, Volatile Linament and Black Salves. Seventy-five cents would get you a bottle of Blood Syrup; for one dollar, you could get Woman's Friend or Lung Syrup.

The leaflet included the names of ninety-nine patients who were willing to offer references for Sleeping Lucy.

But Lucy also had her doubters. In mocking the gullibility of investors in a fictitious silver mine in Brandon, a contributor to the 1877 *Vermont Historical Gazetteer* took a swipe at her in an essay entitled "Credulity": "How is it that two itinerant and perhaps imbecile vagrants have…drawn a rich revenue from the pockets of independent and respectable citizens of this immediate neighborhood, returning naught but the sleeping insane mutterings of a modern Pythoness, [named] 'Sleeping Lucy.'"

Lucy's later years seem to have been difficult ones. She fell into debt. Some blamed Raddin. Perhaps the market for "clairvoyant physicians" had simply dried up. In her mid-seventies, Lucy seems to have contracted colon cancer. Nearing the end, she suffered severely—the illness, however, seems to have helped her reconcile with her daughter. Julia Ann nursed Lucy during this, her final illness, one for which she could find no cure.

16

COUNTING ON WATER CURES

S omething was wrong with Harriet Beecher Stowe.
   She felt down in her spirits. Perhaps, people suggested, she was suffering from melancholia—today we might say she was depressed. So she did what anyone with the means in the mid-nineteenth century would do: she took the water cure.

The popular therapy involved drinking and bathing in spring water. For her treatment, Stowe—who a few years later would write *Uncle Tom's Cabin*—picked the most exclusive, or at least the most expensive, facility of her day, the Brattleboro Hydropathic Institution. The state-of-the-art establishment drew thousands of wealthy people to Vermont, as well as luminaries like Stowe and the poet Henry Wadsworth Longfellow. In Brattleboro, patients were treated for cancer, epilepsy, asthma, dropsy, sweating hands, bunions, scrofula…and the list goes on.

The other seemingly endless list is the one of supposedly curative springs that sprang up in Vermont in time to catch the water-cure fad that raged in the 1840s and '50s.

Clarendon, Newbury, Sheldon, Tunbridge, Middletown, Manchester, Alburg, Highgate, Wheelock, Hardwick, Woodstock, Brunswick, Quechee—every community seemed able to find some water for which to charge people to use.

For their part, patients didn't seem to mind parting with their money. The cure, they thought, was worth it. One patient wrote in a testimonial that "in using less than a case of water procured from your company, my whole system has been benefited and my headache well nigh cured." Another man wrote,

"Waters you supplied have unleashed passions of great magnitude." Even the makers of Viagra don't make that claim.

But this was the nineteenth century. There was no Food and Drug Administration, so hydrotherapy practitioners could make any claim they liked. And the public, eager for cures, was ready to believe them.

The water cure was applied to seemingly any malady. Harriet Beecher Stowe's treatment for mental unrest was typical. She was awakened at 4:00 a.m. and wrapped from head to toe in thick wool blankets. When she was drenched in sweat, she was seated in front of an open window, her head exposed. Then she was plunged, still wrapped in her blankets, into a cold bath.

As Stowe described it, she would "let all the waves and billows roll over me till every limb ached with cold and my hands would scarcely have feeling enough to dress me."

After that, she dried herself, dressed and went on a strenuous walk before sitting down to a cold breakfast. Then came bouts of vigorous exercise interspersed with plunges into cold, often icy, streams. During the course of the day, she was expected to drink from twenty to thirty tumblers of water. For the pleasure of these painful treatments, she paid the exorbitant fee of ten dollars a day (eleven dollars in the summer). The cost would normally have been beyond her means, but friends helped raise the money for her eleven-month stay.

Harriet Beecher Stowe (*pictured*) and Henry Wadsworth Longfellow were among the prominent Americans to seek cures in Brattleboro. *Library of Congress.*

Stowe's doctor was Robert Wesselhoeft, a German immigrant who had studied hydrotherapy from Vincent Priessnitz, an Austrian and one of the leaders of the movement in Europe. Priessnitz had used water immersion to cure himself after being trampled by a horse as a teenager. But the use of water as a treatment is much older. It dates back at least to 500 BC, when Hippocrates—the Greek for whom the medical oath is named—recommended it to treat a variety of ailments, including pneumonia.

The theory behind hydrotherapy, according to one of its leading nineteenth-century practitioners, Dr. Russell Trall, was that by wrapping patients in wet blankets, the impure water in their blood would pass through the skin and be replaced by the pure water in the sheet.

Trall wrote that the treatment "was not a universal cure, as diseases are not universally curable, [but] it was a remedy universally applicable."

But it wasn't a remedy universally accepted. In 1845, the *Boston Medical and Surgical Journal* wrote that healers who "had not succeeded in regular practice, in homeopathy, animal magnetism, pathetism, in the use of purgative pills, temperance bitters, galvanic rings, in thermoelectric practice, Beachism, Thomsonism, Grahamism or any other of the known modes of mongrel practice, have become thorough converts to the water cure."

The first Vermonter to promote the water cure was George Round, who said he found a spring in Clarendon after dreaming of it. Not to overlook the commercial possibilities of his aquifer, Round built a log-cabin inn on the spot. He was well ahead of his time. Round found the spring in 1776. By 1798, a hotel had replaced the cabin.

Similar things happened in other towns. Of the 126 named springs in Vermont in the late nineteenth century, 31 attracted hotels. Some had more than one. Sheldon, which, like many communities, appended the word "Springs" to its name as a marketing tool, boasted as many as ten hotels.

The water-cure craze was a developer's dream. Residents of the Northeast Kingdom town of Wheelock knew about the spring in the center of town, though they mostly ignored it. When they referred to it at all, they called it the "Stinking Spring." But a businessman from Boston named Royal Winter took one whiff and smelled money. Winter bought the Brick Hotel in town and renamed it the Caledonia Mineral Springs Hotel. He renovated the place and piped spring water into the rooms.

But the spring was Winter's downfall. The water quickly lost its sulfur taste, which was a bad thing from a business perspective. Guests liked their water fetid; the smellier the water, the stronger its curative powers, they believed. Worse yet, the water in Wheelock corroded the copper pipes.

A few miles east, in Brunswick, entrepreneur A.J. Congden bought the town's six springs and named each one. He called them Iron Spring, Calcium Spring, Magnesium Spring, White Sulphur Spring, Bromine Spring and Arsenic Spring. By administering them in different doses and sequences, he claimed he could cure a variety of ailments. Unfortunately, all of the water came from the same source.

Despite the quackery associated with the water cure, it seems to have helped some patients. Stowe was happy enough with her stay in Brattleboro that her husband soon sought help there, too. And though it didn't cure Longfellow's eyes as he'd hoped, he was sure the treatment would have done the trick if he had stayed longer. In reviewing more than five hundred cases he'd treated, Dr. Wesselhoeft included two he couldn't cure, just to show that the treatment didn't help everyone.

If many people believed that the treatment improved their health, what's to account for the successes of this bizarre therapy? Scholars believe it helped by getting many patients out of the polluted cities where they lived. It also forced the wealthy, who were used to eating large amounts of fatty foods, to follow a sparse diet and to exercise. There may also have been a placebo (or perhaps a high-price-tag) effect. "If I'm paying all this money," patients may have thought, "the cure has to be doing me some good, right?"

Positive reports weren't the only thing that drew people to the water cure. They also tried it for social reasons: hydrotherapy was in. Anyone who was anyone found a reason to take the cure. When not having various forms of water torture inflicted upon them, patients found time to socialize. In fact, Wesselhoeft had to write in his advertisements that his center was for medical treatment, not entertainment.

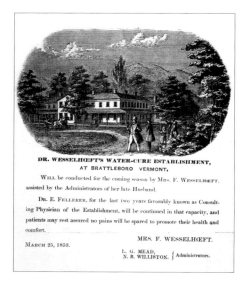

DR. WESSELHŒFT'S WATER-CURE ESTABLISHMENT, AT BRATTLEBORO VERMONT,

WILL be conducted for the coming season by MRS. F. WESSELHŒFT, assisted by the Administrators of her late Husband.

DR. E. FELLERER, for the last two years favorably known as Consulting Physician of the Establishment, will be continued in that capacity, and patients may rest assured no pains will be spared to promote their health and comfort.

MRS. F. WESSELHŒFT.

MARCH 25, 1853.

L. G. MEAD, N. B. WILLISTON. } Administrators.

Robert Wesselhoeft's widow, Ferdinanda, kept his water-cure clinic open after his death in 1852. *Vermont Archives.*

Eventually, like all fads, this one faded. The wealthy began to gravitate toward other pursuits, like walking, automobiles and water sports (boats, not baths). Dr. Wesselhoeft and his hydrotherapy institute didn't live to see the decline. The doctor fell ill in 1851. It couldn't have helped his business in Vermont that he sought medical help in Germany rather than from his own hydropathic clinic. Wesselhoeft died the next year. His widow, Ferdinanda, continued to run the institute, but it closed a few years later.

By the late nineteenth century, most of Vermont's water-cure centers had closed. Many seem to have closed when their hotels burned, which is ironic considering how much water they had lying about. The spa towns that hung on, notably Woodstock and Manchester, offered guests other diversions, like golf, which some visitors found more appealing than being dunked in cold water.

17

OUR CANADIAN PRESIDENT?

As desperate political tactics go, this one has a long history. If you have no other way to defeat a presidential rival, or want to delegitimize a sitting president, then point to the Constitution and claim he is really a foreigner, or at least foreign born, and therefore ineligible to serve. The ploy dates back at least as far as 1880 to Vermont's own Chester A. Arthur. Or perhaps he was Canada's own. That was the charge leveled against the man who would become the twenty-first president.

When Arthur was accused of not being a natural-born American citizen, he was at a disadvantage. Whereas politicians today can produce hard evidence, like state-issued birth certificates and decades-old newspaper birth announcements, Arthur had little but his word. Given the location of his birth near the Canadian border, his ill-conceived decision to fudge his true birth date and the hardball politics of his day, it is little wonder his rivals claimed he had been born in Canada.

The official version of Arthur's birth is that he was born in 1830 in Fairfield, Vermont, a couple of towns south of the Canadian border. He certainly spent his early years in Fairfield, but the question involved where he drew his first breath. If he had been born across the border in Quebec, the Constitution would disqualify him from becoming president or even vice president.

The alleged changing of facts surrounding Arthur's birth was no mere accident, political opponents claimed, but a deliberate conspiracy to skirt the law. Arthur didn't help matters by claiming, apparently out of vanity, to have been born in 1830, while his family Bible, housed at the Library of Congress, states he was born a year earlier.

The proof of Arthur's supposed alien birth was unearthed by Arthur P. Hinman, a New York City lawyer and Democratic political operative. When Arthur was nominated to be the Republican vice-presidential candidate in 1880 (James Garfield was the party's presidential candidate), Hinman snapped into action, traveling to Franklin County to do some sleuthing. Hinman soon claimed that he had discovered that Arthur had been born in Dunham, Quebec, at his grandparents' home, not in Fairfield. (Hinman had previously claimed that Arthur had actually been born in Ireland and had moved to the United States as a teenager.)

Hinman theorized that Arthur had taken as his own the birthplace of a brother who had died in infancy. The politician had been born William Chester Alan Arthur, Hinman wrote, the oldest of three boys in a family that apparently had little imagination for names. A second son, Chester Abell Arthur, died in infancy. When a third boy was born and named William Arthur Jr., the future president dropped the William from his name. Having a deceased brother may have proved expedient for Arthur, at least according to Hinman. The investigator claimed that when Arthur considered running for national office, he expropriated his younger brother's records that showed

he was born in Fairfield. Chester Abell had no death records, Hinman alleged, because his father sold the infant's body to a medical school. Immediately after the nomination, he claimed, Arthur and some aides traveled to Fairfield and elsewhere to create a paper trail showing he was a natural-born American.

The requirement that a president be a "natural born citizen" has been with us from the start. The prerequisite was included in the Constitution in order to prevent foreigners, who may have allegiances to other countries, from holding office. The legal definition of "natural born" American has long been debated but never decided in court. Still, no president has ever been elected who was born outside of the United States.

Political rivals claimed that Chester Arthur was born in Canada, making him ineligible to serve as president. *Library of Congress.*

Unless, of course, you believe that Hinman, despite his political motives, was right. Rumors of a Canadian birth didn't stop the public from electing the Garfield-Arthur ticket in the fall of 1880. But the talk refused to die, thanks in part to an uncharacteristic lapse of judgment by Arthur. Afterward, people were left to wonder whether he was confiding the truth to his supporters or merely poking fun at a baseless rumor he just couldn't shake.

Basking in the victory, and after perhaps too many celebratory drinks, Arthur gave an indiscreet speech at Delmonico's restaurant in New York City. Before a crowd of supporters, including millionaires John Jacob Astor, J. Pierpont Morgan and Jay Gould, Arthur joked about his origins. "[W]hile I don't mean to say anything about my birthplace, whether it was in Canada or elsewhere, still, if I should get to going about the secrets of the campaign, there is no saying what I might say to make trouble between now and the 4th of March [inauguration day]."

On July 2, 1881, an assassin shot President Garfield, who lingered for two months before dying, making Arthur president. A.P. Hinman saw an opportunity to breathe new life into his pet cause. Either out of conviction or to weaken the rival political party—or just to make a few bucks—Hinman published a book, *How a British Subject Became President*. As much as Hinman tried to revive the issue, he failed. With only newspapers to spread his claims, he had trouble convincing the American people the president was a Canadian.

18

AN ISLAND FOR THE FAMOUS

The islanders jealously guarded their privacy. When a group of tourists made the mistake of pulling their boat onto the private land for a picnic, they were accosted by one of the inhabitants. It is hard to say what was most frightening about the man—his unintelligible screaming, the ax he carried or his strange attire. He wore a red wig and nothing else, unless you count the mud smeared across his body.

The tourists couldn't understand his shouts, but they got the message. They quickly clambered back into their boat and left the island behind. Once they had gone, the naked man found his fellow islanders and repeated the story that has been told in those parts ever since. He was part of a clan of avid storytellers who made the island their home each summer for two decades starting in the 1920s.

His name was Harpo Marx. He and other famous actors, writers and artists adopted the island, Neshobe Island in the middle of Lake Bomoseen in Castleton, as their private refuge. "The thing we cherished…along with its natural beauty, was its isolation," Harpo later wrote, which helps explain why the comedy film star would go to such lengths to protect it.

The island was discovered, as far as the celebrities were concerned, by Alexander Woollcott. Little remembered today, Woollcott was perhaps the most influential literary critic of his day, and he knew seemingly everybody, from politicians to movie stars. Woollcott first saw the eight-acre island in 1924 with his financial advisor, who owned Neshobe and wanted to sell it. Woollcott instantly decided it would be the ideal summer retreat for his famous friends. He was a member of the Algonquin Round Table, an informal group of New York City's literati and glitterati who met daily for long lunches and wickedly witty conversation at the Algonquin Hotel. The public knew of their sharp-edged banter, because it frequently ended up in the newspaper columns of journalists who were members. It was here that writer Dorothy Parker, told that the famously staid Vermonter Calvin Coolidge had died, is said to have remarked, "How can they tell?"

Woollcott convinced some of his Algonquin friends to form the Neshobe Island Club and buy most of the island. From the start, Woollcott dominated island life. He eventually paid off the mortgage, giving him ownership of half the island, and in 1937, he built a large stone house on its highest point. Owners and guests not staying at the Stone House, as it was known, lived in the Club House.

Life on the island was primitive at first. Any bathing was done with cold water, a pitcher and a basin, or in the lake. Other basic amenities included outhouses, kerosene lamps and wood stoves. Many club members preferred things simple. But a debate flared between the so-called Masses (who wanted to keep things simple) and the Classes (who wanted modern amenities). The Classes won and brought the luxuries of running water and refrigeration to the island.

There to enjoy the amenities were celebrities such as actors Laurence Olivier, Helen Hayes, Vivien Leigh and Ruth Gordon; writers Noel Coward, Ring Lardner, Thornton Wilder, Robert Benchley and Margaret Mitchell; composer Irving Berlin; and entertainment magnate Walt Disney. Many were just visiting—a single invitation from Woollcott meant nomination to his "Who's Who" list, quipped Harpo; a second invite meant you had made it. The ultimate honor, Harpo said, was membership in the island club, which he himself earned.

Woollcott dictated the day's routine. He insisted that guests greet the day with a dip in the lake, no matter how cold it was, before coming to breakfast, which was served at seven o'clock. Breakfasts stretched on for hours, Algonquin style, with lots of animated conversation and Woollcott reading aloud his daily mail.

Despite Woollcott's rules, much about island life was informal. Some club members and guests preferred to spend much of the day nude. Once, Dorothy Parker showed up for a visit carrying a hatbox. Some days, the gardening hat it contained was all she wore. Harpo had greeted the island's invaders naked because he had been skinny-dipping when he spotted them.

Literary critic Alexander Woollcott, seen posing with actress Gina Malo in his home on Neshobe Island, drew numerous celebrities to Vermont. *New York Public Library.*

The Algonquin crowd was a competitive lot, always trying to one-up each other's latest quip. They brought that competitiveness with them to Neshobe. It showed up particularly in their cutthroat games of croquet, in which players took particular glee in knocking their opponents' balls into the lake.

Harpo wrote in his autobiography about a particularly hard-fought game with Woollcott. At one point, Harpo wanted to smash his ball into Woollcott's, but a maple tree stood in the way. Undeterred, Harpo took an old tire that had been used as a boat bumper, sawed it in half and laid half of it around the tree. Harpo then slammed his ball into the tire, around the tree and into Woollcott's. Woollcott reacted by slamming his mallet into the ground and storming off into his house.

The other regular game was called "Murder," which was played during cocktails. It began with players drawing lots to see who would be the murderer and who would be the district attorney. While the district attorney announced himself or herself, the murderer's identity remained a secret. During cocktails, the murderer would wait for the moment to strike, then discreetly say to his or her victim "You are dead." The victim would then stand motionless until others noticed. The district attorney would question the other partygoers to reveal the murderer.

One night, when Woollcott was the district attorney, no murder victim had turned up by the time dinner was ready. Someone noticed that one of the guests, author Alice Duer Miller, was missing. Woollcott refused to allow dinner to be served before the case was cracked. Club members and guests scoured the house and turned up nothing. Finally, at 11:00 p.m., a club member spied Miller through the keyhole of the back bathroom. Hours earlier, Miller had gone in to use the bathroom and found the words "YOU ARE DED," complete with misspelling, written in red lipstick on the toilet paper. Miller had gamely played her part and remained in the bathroom. Woollcott instantly knew whose work this was. Without asking any questions,

Comic actor Harpo Marx, pictured here in a movie poster wearing his trademark curly wig, was a mainstay on Neshobe Island. *Wikimedia Commons.*

he wheeled on Harpo and declared him the murderer, then berated him for breaking the rules by not speaking the words to his victim.

The island's celebrities, and their unorthodox behavior, spawned rumors and gossip. Some have claimed that every home on Lake Bomoseen was sure to contain binoculars to watch this exotic wildlife. But apart from Harpo's naked wild-man act, relations between the island's inhabitants and those on the mainland seem to have been cordial. Local residents often worked for the club, ferrying guests, groceries and messages to the island. Others worked as handymen or cooks. The only locals who visited the island uninvited were ice fishermen, who would rest there occasionally in the winter when the New Yorkers had returned home.

Club members and guests didn't just play on the island. Some found it a source of inspiration. Book manuscripts were completed there, as was part of the screenplay for the movie adaptation of *Wuthering Heights*. Stage actresses walked around the island, rehearsing lines for upcoming productions.

The Neshobe Island Club faded with the health of its founder, Woollcott, who suffered a series of heart attacks. At one point, Woollcott quipped that on doctor's orders he was only allowed to play croquet if he were permitted to win. Woollcott died in New York City in 1943, hours after suffering a heart attack during a live broadcast of his weekly radio show *The Town Crier*.

The next day, a group of Castleton residents marked his death by issuing a statement that they would "long remember with deep appreciation the many benefactions of Alexander Woollcott." During his years on the island, Woollcott had not held himself aloof from the town. In fact, he had taken the time to serve as a trustee for the town library and had donated many review copies of books he received.

Woollcott had requested that his ashes be buried at his alma mater, Hamilton College in New York State. Harpo commented that a more fitting tribute would be for them to be "blown through the fifth wicket of the Neshobe Island croquet ground."

PART IV
PERSONAL STRUGGLE AND SOCIAL ACTIVISM

19

THE ABENAKI'S DILEMMA

W hat can be more terrifying than living in a society descending into chaos on the brink of civil war? As tensions rise, you hear neighbors testing their weapons as they arm themselves against one another. On which side will you fight? Or will you try to avoid the fighting somehow? Fortunately, this situation is far from what we experience today in Vermont, but that hasn't always been the case.

Imagine for a moment you are an Abenaki living in Vermont at the outbreak of the Revolutionary War. Suddenly you are living in the midst of two warring groups and faced with a difficult decision: will you back the British or the rebelling American colonists? This dilemma faced the Abenaki in the late 1770s, when the war's outcome was far from certain.

Native Americans, who had arrived in the region at least twelve thousand years earlier, had had to choose sides ever since Europeans first appeared in significant numbers in the early 1600s. For the century and a half since then, the Abenaki had backed the French against the British.

Choosing the French in that earlier dispute was perhaps easier than picking sides in the American Revolution. When the French arrived in Canada, they came well armed, with a plan to establish colonies there, and eventually started moving into the Champlain Valley. The alternative to finding an accommodation with the French would probably have meant fighting them. Besides, why not side with the French? After all, they were offering to help the Algonquin tribes, which included the Abenaki, defeat their longtime foes, the Iroquois. The French wanted to ally with the Algonquin to gain a large piece of the region's fur trade.

From the perspective of the French, the Algonquin proved to be valuable allies throughout numerous wars that rocked the Northeast and Canada, starting with King Philip's War (1675–77) and not concluding until five wars later, with the French and Indian War (1754–63). That last war ended with a major French defeat, which meant they were finished as a political and military force in North America, though of course many French people continued to make their homes in Canada.

Although the fighting had stopped, the era brought fresh challenges to the Abenaki of Vermont. Peace brought a sense of stability that encouraged British colonists to move north into Vermont, where land was cheap, plentiful and no longer sitting on the fault line between warring nations. Suddenly, settlements sprang up seemingly everywhere.

Which colony owned the land that is today Vermont was much in debate, with New York and New Hampshire making forceful claims. By 1764, New Hampshire's governor had issued charters to 112 towns in the area then known as the New Hampshire Grants. Not to be outdone, New York issued competing charters. By the mid-1770s, the two neighboring colonies had issued grants to roughly 3.5 million of Vermont's 5.9 million acres.

Issuing grants wasn't the same as actually settling the land, but thousands of colonists from Massachusetts and Connecticut, and some as far away as Scotland, did move north into Vermont, believing it was their right to do so. The land had, in fact, belonged for untold generations to the indigenous people. But by the 1770s, the indigenous population of Vermont had been drastically reduced by epidemics and warfare. Those who remained found their ancestral lands being encroached on by growing numbers of British settlers. The population of the Grants soared from roughly four hundred settlers in 1762 to twenty thousand in 1775.

Peace lasted barely a dozen years. When hostilities erupted again, the situation baffled some Abenaki. They were used to the British and French hating each other, but this war, a sort of civil war pitting a country and its own colonists against one another, was bizarre. As one Abenaki woman said, "O strange English men kill one another. I think the world is coming to an end."

Not surprisingly, individual Abenaki made different choices in deciding how to deal with this chaotic world. Some backed the British, while others supported the Americans. And many more tried to remain neutral, since this wasn't their fight.

During the American Revolution, both the British and the Americans viewed the Abenaki as a valuable ally. *Wikimedia Commons*.

But staying neutral proved difficult, because Vermont played a strategic role in the Revolutionary War. The British military in Canada viewed the Champlain Valley as the best invasion route. In addition, the rebel stronghold at Newbury in the Upper Connecticut River Valley (known by the Abenaki as Coos or Cowass) was also a concern for the British.

Both sides viewed Vermont's Abenaki population as an important ally and tried to win them over. The British offered the Abenaki favorable trading terms and promised that they could keep their ancestral lands. American colonists offered trade and military protection.

Each side won converts. Abenaki warriors were among the Native Americans who fought with the British in the unsuccessful defense of St. John, in Quebec, and the successful defense of Montreal. They also helped the British defeat the American force at Valcour Island on Lake Champlain in 1776. Other Abenaki warriors, however, joined General George Washington's forces, laying siege to British-held Boston, and fought with the Americans during their failed invasion of Quebec.

Word of that spectacular American defeat at Quebec terrified Vermont settlers. The American army was in full retreat, carrying smallpox with it and being pursued by British troops and by warriors from several tribes. The townspeople of Newbury strengthened their fortifications and braced for an assault. The news also frightened local Abenaki, who sought refuge in the settlers' blockhouses. When an attack failed to materialize, the settlers and Abenaki left the safety of the blockhouses, perhaps realizing that, sometimes, their fates were connected.

General Jacob Bayley and others viewed the Abenaki as an important buffer against a British attack on the upper valley. Bayley said he would match the trading terms offered by the British, because "if the Indians trade with us we need no Soldiers."

In July 1777, a group of forty-five Abenaki families left Canada for the New Hampshire Grants, seeking to settle somewhere north of Newbury. An American general said the Abenaki could stay and ordered local officers to settle them near the American settlement. They wouldn't have to fight in the current military campaign, the general wrote, but "we Expect that they hold themselves in readiness to give us their aid should it be wanted in the next."

Throughout the war, the loyalty of Abenaki living in Vermont shifted as events unfolded. Their fluid allegiance drove the British and the Americans to distraction. The British grumbled that the Abenaki just picked whichever side they believed was strongest; the Americans had similar complaints.

How did the British and the Americans think the Abenaki should decide whom to support? Did they expect the Abenaki to be motivated by loyalty, to a cause that wasn't their own? Whatever side they chose to back, it must have been an excruciating decision in a dangerous and chaotic world—one that was about to change for this region's Native Americans forever.

20

Ann Story

Resolution in Revolution

L ike so many of their Connecticut neighbors, Amos and Hannah Story decided their prospects would be better in the largely unsettled territory that lay between Lake Champlain and the Connecticut River. The region, then known as the New Hampshire Grants, was contested by its adjacent colonies, New Hampshire and New York. Because of the uncertain validity of any land grants issued by the two colonies, parcels in the Grants were much less expensive than land in southern New England. The Storys' decision to settle in the Grants had tragic consequences for the family, but it also produced one of the first heroes in what would become Vermont.

Remembered today as Ann Story, the hero began life as Hannah Reynolds in Preston, Connecticut. After marrying, she and Amos had five children. In 1774, Amos set off for the Grants with the oldest of those children, thirteen-year-old Solomon. The two built a cabin on land the Storys had acquired in the town of Salisbury. Then tragedy struck. While the father and son were clearing the surrounding forest, a large maple tree two feet in diameter spun unpredictably and fell on Amos. Solomon frantically tried to chop through the trunk to free his father, refusing to believe Amos was dead. Finally, Solomon accepted the truth, and with the help of distant neighbors he had summoned, he buried Amos.

Solomon faced another horrible task. He had to make the long walk to tell his mother and siblings what had happened. The family had probably moved into the Grants, to Rutland, by this time, though one account says they were still in Connecticut. We don't know how Ann Story bore the news, but we do know what she did next. She made one of those decisions that seem to make sense only in fables. With or without a husband, she decided to stick with her plans. Amos had braved the wilderness with the help of Solomon and had died. Now Ann would head into the wilds, and she'd do it with five children in tow. On their way north, the family visited Amos's grave, then trudged on to the small cabin in Salisbury, which sat beside Otter Creek.

There the family settled into the rigors of life on the frontier, with Story setting the example for her children. As town historian John Weeks, who knew Story late in her life, wrote: "She was resolute, determined, and fearless.…Fearless of savage beasts or savage men. She was in possession of good health and an iron constitution. She could use the axe equal to most pioneers."

Weeks, writing in 1860, portrayed a world that must have seemed far fiercer than his own and told of the Storys' ordeal. "Here, the wolf, the bear, and other beasts of prey made their midnight howls," he wrote, "here, the savages roamed and stalked abroad; and here, within 15 months from her introduction to this wilderness country, her dwelling, though humble, was laid in ashes by the savage foes."

The fire happened in the spring of 1776, after the onset of the Revolutionary War. Parties of Indians, working with their British allies, had begun burning settlers' homes in the area. The attacks were so feared that most families had abandoned their homesteads for safer places like Rutland. The Storys were in fact the only family left in the area. One morning, one of Story's children noticed smoke rising from the vacant house of their nearest neighbor. Realizing their home might be next, Story and her children quickly grabbed precious possessions—blankets, utensils, a kettle, maple sugar and bear grease—loaded their canoe and paddled away. The family pulled the boat into a nearby thicket and watched as Indians raided their cabin and burned it to the ground.

A less strong-willed person would have done the sensible thing: packed up and moved out of the woods and back to the town of Rutland. But Story demonstrated a trait still associated with Vermonters: stubbornness. She and her children rebuilt the cabin, constructing it out of poles rather than logs, since that was all the younger children could handle.

Ann Story might have been headstrong, but she was also smart. The family would no longer sleep in the cabin. Instead, she and the children carved a cave into the far bank of the creek. The cave's mouth, at water level and covered by bushes, was only big enough to accommodate a canoe

Widow Ann Story is famed for showing great bravery while defending her children during the perilous days of the American Revolution. *National Life Group*.

with its occupants lying down. Inside, though, it was larger, with room for the family to sleep on shelves and, reportedly, enough space to store supplies for the Green Mountain Boys.

Story did what she could to help the revolutionaries. The homestead was said to be a way station for the rebels, a place to pass along messages or to pick up vital information about the movements of British troops or Tories, supporters of the king. Story, some historians say, was a friend of Ethan Allen, the leader of the Green Mountain Boys, and his spy.

Legend has it that Story once returned home to find the door barred by someone from the inside. Seeing a group of Tories nearby, she realized it wasn't one of them. They asked her who was in the house. She said no one. She locked the door, she explained, to keep animals and Indians out and would reenter through a hole in the roof. As the Tories watched, Story climbed a ladder, pulled back a piece of bark from the roof and dropped inside. There, she found what she'd half expected: a party of Green Mountain Boys taking refuge.

The family apparently adapted to spending nights in their cave, so much so that they soon took in a stranger, a pregnant young woman whom Solomon had found crying in the forest. The woman had been captured by an Indian raiding party and made to march toward Quebec. Being late in her pregnancy, she fell behind and was left to starve. She was lucky not to have been killed, the fate of most captives who lagged.

Story helped deliver the baby and invited the mother and child to sleep in the cave.

Soon afterward, a local man named Ezekiel Jenny was walking along Otter Creek at night on his way to a meeting with perhaps three dozen other Tories. The group was headed to Canada to provide the British army with information about the defenses of Vermont's guerrilla fighters. Jenny heard a baby crying on the far side of the creek. Curious, he hid and waited until morning, when Ann and the others pushed the bushes aside and paddled out. Jenny had solved the mystery of where the Storys went at night. But then Jenny made a mistake: he tried to get more information from Story. When the canoe landed near the family's cabin, he stepped forward, leveled his rifle at her and demanded details about the rebels.

"I gave evasive and dissatisfactory replies to his answers," she later explained. "This exasperated Jenny and he threatened to shoot me on the spot; but to all his threats I bid defiance, and told him I had no fears of being shot by so consummate a coward as he."

Aggravated, Jenny stomped off to meet his fellow Tories. Story saw another chance to help the Revolution. She tore the flyleaf from her Bible, the only paper she had at hand, and dashed off a note about her clash with Jenny. She sent Solomon to run and deliver it to the nearest Green Mountain Boys.

Solomon proved as brave and competent as his mother. He delivered the note and soon joined a posse of a dozen rebels racing north to intercept the Tories. They caught up with them in Monkton and easily captured the Tories while they slept. The men admitted their plot and were marched off as prisoners to Fort Ticonderoga. It was a major counterintelligence coup that helped save the Green Mountain Boys from attack.

What would have happened to the Green Mountain Boys without Ann Story? And what of Vermont history? It would lack one of its greatest heroes, one whose contribution is representative of the sacrifices made by so many forgotten female Patriots.

21

A Black Preacher's Rise
to Prominence

To say the odds were stacked against Lemuel Haynes from birth is an understatement. Here are some of the obstacles that stood in the way of his eventually finding his calling as one of Vermont's—indeed New England's—most highly regarded preachers: First, he was illegitimate. His birth on July 18, 1753, in West Hartford, Connecticut, was the accidental result of a tryst. Second, he never knew his father, whose name has been lost to history.

Third, he never really knew his mother, either. Her identity has been debated for two and a half centuries. One theory is that she was a Scottish immigrant servant named Lucy Fitch who worked for the Haynes family of West Hartford. Others suggest that Fitch was merely a convenient (and perhaps not entirely willing) stand-in for the boy's true mother. According to this theory, his mother was a Goodwin, a member of a prominent Hartford family who had sought refuge from scandal in the Haynes household.

Fourth, on the baby's birth, people learned that the father was black. The baby could have been born in worse situations at the time—New England was by colonial American standards a tolerant place—but his mixed-race parentage would forever be a burden.

After Fitch attested that she was the mother, the Haynes family fired her. As a way to give the boy a respectable name, or as revenge against her former employer, she gave the baby the last name of Haynes. So it was that Lemuel Haynes greeted the world.

No one seemed to want this unintended baby. Fitch left him behind when she left the Haynes house. The Hayneses didn't want to raise him, either, so they gave him to a farming family, the Roses. They were traveling through West Hartford on their way to settling in the town of Granville, Massachusetts. He wasn't treated like family; he was made an indentured servant until he turned twenty-one.

But critically for Haynes's future, the Roses treated him as one of their own in terms of education. They encouraged him to read and study whenever he found the time and sent him to school with their other children on the rare occasions they attended classes.

The Reverend Lemuel Haynes was the first African American to receive an honorary degree. *New York Public Library*.

The head of the household, Deacon David Rose, learned to rely on Haynes's intelligence and judgment. By the time Haynes was a teen, he was entrusted with the difficult task of dealing with horse traders. And at many Sunday dinners, he was called upon to restate the sermon he had heard that day for the benefit of family members who attended another church.

Just as Deacon Rose came to appreciate his surrogate son, Haynes learned to admire the deacon's devotion to God and sought to emulate it. Haynes's religious fervor was coupled with fear, the fear that he would die a sinner. One night, he saw northern lights and dreaded they foretold Judgment Day. "For many days and nights I was greatly alarmed for fear of appearing before the bar of God, knowing that I was a sinner," he later wrote. Soon afterward, he had himself baptized.

After turning twenty-one, Haynes left Granville to serve briefly as a minuteman in the Boston area at the start of the Revolutionary War. In 1776, he helped reinforce Fort Ticonderoga against a feared British attack, which didn't end up coming until the next year, after Haynes had returned home to recuperate from typhus.

Haynes focused again on religion, studying Greek, Latin and sermon writing with a pair of ministers in Connecticut. He completed his studies in 1780. Immediately, the parishioners of a new Congregational church in Granville called him to be their preacher, thus making him the first African American ever to lead an all-white congregation. Five years later, he became the first black person ordained by any religious organization in North America.

Haynes's position as preacher soon offered him further recognition from the white community. One of his parishioners, Elizabeth Babbit, became an admirer and asked him to marry her. His being part black made it impossible for him to ask her. After consulting his fellow preachers to gauge the reaction of other whites, Haynes accepted.

He soon had another proposal to ponder. In 1787, Haynes had served on a preaching circuit that took him into what was then the Republic of Vermont. His firm and ardent sermons caught people's attention. Whether out of racial tolerance or due to the shortage of preachers on the frontier, the members of the West Parish congregation in West Rutland asked Haynes to lead them. Haynes would lead them for thirty years.

That didn't mean he found universal acceptance. One church member years later recalled being taunted by boys from another church who mocked Haynes as a "nigger preacher." Whatever insults he endured, Haynes was a success. Under his leadership, the West Rutland congregation grew from forty-six members to more than three hundred. People remembered him for his quick, if sometimes acerbic, wit. When another minister's papers were lost in a fire, Haynes supposedly suggested that they had produced more light in the blaze than they ever had from the pulpit. Another time, two boys shouted to him in the street, "Father Haynes, have you heard the good news? The Devil is dead!" Haynes patted the boys on the head and said, "Oh, you poor fatherless children! What will become of you?"

But in church, Haynes seldom joked. An acquaintance said, "When he ascended the pulpit, it was with a gravity which seemed to indicate that he felt the amazing weight of his charge as an ambassador of God to dying men." A fellow minister said, "His enunciation, though remarkably clear, was extremely rapid; a delightful flow of words and thoughts, as if they were crowding each other for utterance."

That "delightful flow of words" won Haynes admirers throughout the Northeast. He was regularly invited to be a visiting preacher or to deliver a sermon on Independence Day or Washington's birthday. He received an honorary master's degree from Middlebury College and authored a widely read attack on Universalism and its belief in universal salvation.

After three decades of leading his West Rutland congregation, Haynes sensed he was no longer wanted. He submitted his resignation, and the congregation accepted. Haynes later explained to a friend that after thirty years his congregation had discovered that it had a black preacher. Although racial prejudice might have been the cause, it also might have been a case of a preacher and his congregation growing apart, a common occurrence in early America. Haynes's old-fashioned political and religious beliefs, particularly that only a select few would attain salvation, were at odds with those of the new, younger members of his congregation.

After departing Rutland, Haynes finished his career with a three-year stint in Manchester and another eleven years in South Granville, New York, just over the border from West Pawlet.

Haynes fought his entire life to overcome the disadvantages of his obscure birth and racial prejudice. Despite those struggles, he eventually found broad acceptance in the white world. Perhaps fearing losing that acceptance, Haynes seldom spoke on the most important racial issue of the day: slavery. Although he avoided the subject of race, Haynes's prominence made people in the white community confront the issue at some level every day. As one scholar suggested, his very presence and example made those he knew "better Christians" and better people.

22

VERMONT'S FIRST STRIKE

Vermont had never seen anything like it. Hundreds of laborers simply walked off the job one day. The dispute was over pay—not low pay, but *no* pay. The laborers had received no wages since they started work more than two months earlier. Working conditions might well have been an issue, too; the work these men were doing was dangerous, even deadly at times.

Vermont's first labor strike occurred in July 1846 and involved workers who had been building a railroad trestle and laying track through the town of Bolton. The men were recent arrivals from Ireland, having landed first in Canada, where railroad representatives recruited them. The Irish laborers, some accompanied by their families, had fled their homeland during the Potato Famine, a massive crop failure that would claim more than one million lives.

They must have been grateful to find work in Vermont, but when the promised pay didn't materialize, they surely feared that their families were still in danger. The men launched what was soon dubbed the Bolton War—though that's a bit hyperbolic. What came next could more accurately be called a riot or a protest, depending on your perspective.

The Irish laborers and their families lived in a pair of temporary settlements north of the Winooski River in Bolton. The settlements, nicknamed Cork and Dublin, were home to about three hundred people. You can see the rough location of the shantytowns if you drive through the Bolton Flats area on Interstate 89 or Route 2. The towns were apparently built just north of those roads and crept slightly up the hillsides. The land is privately owned and hasn't been studied by archaeologists.

On or around July 1, 1846, the work camps emptied as roughly two hundred laborers, perhaps joined by their wives and children, marched to the hotel where a railroad manager was staying, in the nearby Jonesville section of Richmond.

Laborers had earlier confronted a low-level contractor named H.S. Barnum to complain about their missing wages. Barnum had said he didn't have the money; they should talk with a Mr. Barker, who was a higher-level contractor. Then, fearing for his life, Barnum fled to Burlington.

Thus it was Barker who faced the angry workers, who swore they would hold him prisoner until they were paid. The situation might not have been Barker's fault; railroad ventures in those days were notoriously corrupt. The principal contractor would subcontract work to others. Those subcontractors would, in turn, contract out their work. The process would be repeated and create more layers of subcontractors, each of whom would skim a bit of the construction money before passing it down.

Barker said he didn't have the funds to pay the workers; he said he had never been paid by the principal contractor, a Mr. Belknap. Belknap, in turn, claimed that the Vermont Central Railroad, the corporation organizing the track construction, owed him $200,000.

But Barker said he could straighten things out if the strikers permitted him to travel to Montpelier. Figuring that Barker was their bargaining chip, the workers refused to let him leave. Barker sent an associate, Stephen Haight, instead.

While awaiting Haight's return, the workers did what they could to get attention for their cause. They encamped around the hotel and made speeches about the injustices they had suffered. "Give us our pay and we will disperse—this is all we ask, and this we will have," they told the local sheriff when he arrived and tried to end the impasse. Strikers had created obstacles in the road that ran between Burlington and Montpelier, and they threatened anyone who tried to pass.

Local resident Edward Jones wrote about the incident to his son, Jebez, who was living out of state: "Recently the R.R. Chaps have had a break up in some way or for some Cause they did not pay their workmen and the Pats [Irishmen] waged a small Mexican war. Shut up one of the directors, stopped Teams on the Road, forbid them to pass, dug ditches across the Road and stopped the stage two hours before they could pass. Their employers ought to have paid them but this state of things Could not be Endured."

Railroad workers lay track near Danville in the mid-1800s. Many of the laborers who built the railroad in Vermont were Irish immigrants. *Vermont Historical Society.*

Haight apparently didn't return as promised, and the blockade continued. The local sheriff arrested several strike leaders, but the men were soon rescued by force. Then the sheriff called for backup. In those days, that meant the militia. The Burlington Light Infantry, along with a company of Burlington firefighters armed by the sheriff with muskets—seventy-five to eighty men in all—arrived on the evening of July 3. If the laborers needed more convincing that their situation was hopeless, a Roman Catholic priest arrived and persuaded the men to give up.

Jones, in his letter to his son, wrote, "The militia were Called out and when the Pats saw them Coming, they fled to the mountains in Bolton." A handful of strikers—estimates vary from nine to twelve—were caught and briefly jailed in Burlington. Despite their protest, the strikers never received their back pay.

In reporting the incident, DeWitt Clinton Clarke, editor of the *Burlington Free Press*, criticized the "outrage" caused by the laborers, but he was also sympathetic to their plight. "Now these were poor men, earning their daily bread by the sweat of their faces, and they ought to have been promptly paid."

Despite the strikers' illegal actions, he wrote, "we yet unhesitatingly affirm that these laborers, indefensible as their conduct became, were not the first wrongdoers. That sin must lie at the doors of those who, knowing their necessities, continued to receive the benefit of their unrewarded labor."

Breaking the strike did little to benefit the railroad, however. "The R.R. to me seems to be a Rather an uphill business," Jones wrote. "Years must pass away before it is Completed."

Indeed, work on the tracks halted for almost three years. Construction resumed in March 1849, and the line was completed by November. The work remained hazardous. Seventeen men lost their lives running track through Bolton. But at least now they and others who took the risks were getting paid.

23

FUROR OVER JOHN BROWN'S BODY

J oshua Young had a train to catch. Aboard it was his hero, the violent abolitionist John Brown—or his body, at least. Brown had been hanged days earlier by the State of Virginia, on December 2, 1859, and now his casket was headed home for burial in upstate New York.

Young shared Brown's hatred of slavery, and both men favored scorched-earth tactics to defeat it. Brown fought with weapons; Young fought with words. As minister of Burlington's Congregational Unitarian Church, Young had used his pulpit to attack slavery. His sermons had drawn admirers but had also made enemies among the church's more conservative members, some of whom owned mills that relied on Southern, slave-picked cotton.

Young was deeply saddened by the news of Brown's death. Brown believed he was God's agent, sent to destroy slavery. He and his followers, including five of his sons, had become famous for brutalizing slave owners in the Kansas Territory while fighting over whether the region would be admitted to the Union as a free or a slave state. They had ended up murdering in the name of abolition, slaughtering five slavery supporters. The killings had turned countless admirers against Brown, but they hadn't swayed Young.

The thirty-seven-year-old minister still supported Brown when he was hanged for attacking the federal arsenal at Harpers Ferry, Virginia, in the misguided belief that he would lead a slave rebellion with the arms he would seize. So Young had an easy time making up his mind when Lucius Bigelow, a friend and fellow abolitionist, stopped Young on a Burlington street and asked whether he would like to attend Brown's funeral.

The Reverend Joshua Young was ostracized by some members of his congregation after he officiated at the funeral of abolitionist John Brown. *University of Vermont Special Collections.*

Though he had never met Brown, Young agreed to meet Bigelow to catch the afternoon train.

Young rushed home to tell his wife his plans. She asked if it was wise to attend the funeral of such a controversial man. "It may not be wise, but I am going anyway," he told her. The response was typical of Young. Since arriving in Burlington in 1852 to lead his church (for which the city's Church Street is named), he had often listened to his heart more than his head. But he understood the risks of following his convictions.

As the new minister, he stated in a sermon that opponents of slavery had been "branded as fanatics, thrown out of office, dismissed from their parishes, politically proscribed, socially ostracized…not in the South, but in the North—in New England, in Massachusetts. God forbid that I should say in Vermont!"

At the time, Vermonters were not uniformly against slavery. In the 1830s, a visiting abolitionist, the Reverend Samuel J. May, was run out of Montpelier by an angry mob. In Young's own church, a sign reading "For colored people" had hung in the corner of the balcony. The congregation was willing to have black people worship with them, but not in the same pews. In a show of growing tolerance, the sign was taken down in 1845, fourteen years before John Brown's death.

But Young's unrestrained hatred of slavery—and perhaps the knowledge that he sometimes sheltered runaway slaves at his Willard Street home—rankled some.

He also got into trouble with abolitionists in town, however, for backing out of an antislavery convention in 1858. Young apparently withdrew because he thought the event was attracting too many followers of free love, Spiritualism and other fringe beliefs. Young offered to resign over the controversy, but his congregation rejected the idea by a vote of forty to two.

Young and Bigelow caught a train south to Vergennes, planning to meet Brown's funeral cortege. They arrived to bad news: the procession was a day ahead of them. Brown's widow and the others had spent the night before at the Bardwell House in Rutland, and at about this time would have been arriving at the family homestead in North Elba, New York.

The men rushed south by carriage to Panton to catch the ferry across Lake Champlain, but by now a nor'easter had blown in, pelting the men with rain and snow. The ferry wasn't going anywhere until the weather cleared, the ferryman announced. No amount of arguing could move him, though Young and Bigelow tried for two hours.

Then, suddenly, the storm passed. With the moon shining brightly, the men were ferried across the lake. Arriving on the New York side after midnight, Young and Bigelow—drenched by now—knocked at a nearby farmhouse where they saw a light and persuaded the farmer to drive them by wagon to the Browns' home. They arrived early the next morning.

Entering the house, Young reported, they found it crowded with family, friends, admirers and freed blacks living in the area "who had personally known and admired the man who had gone forth from them a simple shepherd and now was brought back dead with a fame gone out into all the world."

Wendell Phillips, a leading Boston abolitionist, stepped from the crowd and spoke quietly with Young. "It would give Mrs. Brown and the other widows great satisfaction if you would perform the usual service of a clergyman on this occasion." For all of Brown's fame, or perhaps because of his notoriety, Young was the only clergyman present.

The service inside the farmhouse started at one o'clock. After hymns, prayers and a eulogy by Phillips, the pallbearers brought the casket outside, placed it on a table and opened it so mourners could get a last look at their hero. "It was almost as natural as life," Young would later write. "There was a flush on the face, resulting probably from the peculiar mode of his death, and nothing of the pallor that is usual when life is extinct." At the grave, Young quoted Saint Paul: "I have fought the good fight, I have finished the course." Young later said of that day, "It was a scene of unutterable emotion, of touching pathos....It was the old, old story of the prophet's fate, 'Truth forever on the scaffold, wrong forever on the throne.'"

Word of Young's role in the funeral got back to Burlington about the same time he did.

The *Burlington Sentinel* expressed outrage that Young had used the words of Saint Paul in reference to Brown. The paper wrote: "Was it to sanction

The Reverend Joshua Young's former church still stands at the top of Church Street in Burlington. *Library of Congress.*

publicly [Brown's] murders that the Reverend Joshua donned his sacerdotal robes, left his Master's flock, periled his valuable life by traveling night and day through one of the most tedious storms incident to this northern climate, and united with the infidel [Phillips] in casting pearls before swine and singing praises to the memory of a Felon, over his grave, made premature by his murders?"

Worse than the newspaper's barbs, perhaps, were the snubs. At the next week's Sunday services, Young noticed changes in his congregation. Some new faces appeared in the crowd, and some familiar ones were missing. He sensed "a certain unmistakable indication that things were different."

They were, indeed. He learned what had happened the next day. "Six of the wealthiest families of my parish had taken an oath and gone over to a neighboring church, not a few, of the class that follow in the train of the rich, were equally disaffected. On all sides the arrows of public rebuke began to fly. On the street I observed that old friends seeing me coming, suddenly remembered that they had forgotten something and turned back, or, crossing over passed by on the other side." His congregation, for the most part, had tolerated his abolitionist views. But presiding over the funeral of a murderer was too much.

Young withstood the slights for several years; he still had admirers among the city's abolitionists. But by 1862, the congregation decided it was time for a new minister. At a meeting of the church's men, two-thirds voted that they were "not content" with Young. He immediately tendered his resignation, and this time it was accepted. Some historians believe Young was driven out by mill owners, who were allegedly smuggling in Southern cotton during the Civil War. They theorize that the mill owners feared Young would learn of the smuggling and expose them. Young left the Burlington church in March 1863 for a friendlier congregation in Massachusetts.

Recalling how the city had turned against him for participating in the funeral, Young wrote, "I left Burlington a respected and beloved pastor. I returned to find myself in disgrace, an exile in the place of my residence, and little better than a social outcast. Honorable men there were who suggested that it would be a spectacle not for tears, to see me dangling at the end of a rope from the highest tree on the common, swinging and twisting in the wind."

So, just as John Brown had martyred himself for the cause of freedom, Young had sacrificed his career in Vermont for John Brown.

24

ANARCHISTS VS. SOCIALISTS

A Fight to the Death

In a city full of monuments, two stand out. One reveals the cultural riches that immigrants brought with them to Barre, Vermont, during the late nineteenth and early twentieth centuries; the other reveals the extreme tensions that they also carried with them. Both monuments involve master stone carver Elia Corti. He helped create the first monument; the second marks his grave.

Immigrants flooded Barre during the last two decades of the 1800s, swelling the city's population from roughly two thousand inhabitants to more than ten thousand. Most of the new arrivals were, like Corti, Italian, but many others came from places like Scotland, Ireland, Germany and Canada. They mostly came for work in the city's granite industry. Many labored in the quarries. The more skilled workers gravitated to the granite sheds, where they crafted massive chunks of stone into monuments.

Among the most gifted was Corti. So when members of Barre's Scottish community wanted to erect a monument to their countryman, famed poet Robert Burns, they commissioned Corti and his partner, Samuel Novelli, to do the work. While Novelli carved the likeness of Burns, Corti took on the more intricate panels depicting scenes from Burns's poems that would adorn the monument's base. The resulting work is widely admired within the granite-carving community. At one point, the *New York Times* called Corti the nation's greatest granite carver.

The Robert Burns Memorial stands in front of the former Spaulding Graded School, now home of the Vermont Historical Society. It also stands

Italian immigrants built the Socialist Party Labor Hall in 1900. At the time, the community was known as the "granite capital of the world." *Author's photo.*

as a symbol of what was lost when Corti, only thirty-four years old, was gunned down on October 3, 1903.

That night, noted socialist journalist Giacinto Serrati was scheduled to speak at the city's Socialist Party Labor Hall, which served as a social and cultural hub for the Italian community.

Some saw the visit as inflammatory. Barre was a hotbed for anarchists, and Serrati regularly attacked anarchists in the pages of the Socialist Labor Party's weekly newspaper, *Il Proletario*. In fact, a year earlier, Serrati had visited Barre to debate Luigi Galleani, an internationally known anarchist who lived in the city under an assumed name and published the newspaper *Cronaca Sovversiva* ("Subversive Chronicle"). The city's Italian community was divided between anarchists and socialists—though, presumably, many Italians didn't actively support either faction.

The political activity of the immigrants had brought benefits to workers by defending their rights through the work of unions. By 1900, fully 90 percent of workers in Barre belonged to unions.

The hurly-burly of local politics, however, sometimes triggered violence. In December 1900, anarchists ambushed the local police chief, a sturdy Irishman named Patrick Brown, shooting him in the abdomen; he survived. In a similar attack the following year in Buffalo, an anarchist killed President William McKinley.

Vermont anarchists allegedly planned to disrupt Serrati's talk. He was supposed to speak at seven o'clock. But the hour came and went, and no Serrati. Perhaps he feared for his safety.

Anarchists, who had packed the labor hall in hopes of giving Serrati a rough greeting, began to jeer at the socialists present. The taunts led to a scuffle and, soon, to a full-scale brawl. Men threw punches; one was struck over the head with a chair. "Socialists should be killed," some anarchists supposedly shouted.

At this point, a thirty-nine-year-old socialist named Alessandro Garetto, who had been sitting and waiting for the speaker to arrive, joined the fight. At his subsequent trial, Garetto claimed he had been trying to leave the building when he was attacked. Others claimed he entered the fray willingly.

As he stood in the midst of the brawl, Garetto pulled a pistol from his pocket and fired at least twice. One shot grazed one of the anarchists he was fighting. The other struck Elia Corti in the stomach. Corti slumped to the floor as Garetto charged down the steps and into the night.

What Corti had been doing just before being shot has been debated ever since. Some claim he was among the anarchists in the melee. Some witnesses said Corti had been playing the role of peacemaker. Still others said he had just entered the building when Garetto fired. Corti's political beliefs at the time of the shooting are similarly difficult to reconstruct. After arriving in Barre in 1892, he had served as secretary of the city's anarchist club. But in recent years, as he grew more successful and became the father of three daughters, his interest in politics seems to have waned.

Fearing that a mob would kill him, Garetto ran to the nearby offices of a judge, who turned the frightened man over to the police. Realizing that Garetto was in danger of being lynched, Chief Brown transported him by wagon to the jail in Montpelier. Along the route, Brown had the wagon stop to pick up a patient who needed urgent medical care at Heaton Hospital in Montpelier.

Thus it was that Garetto came face to face with his victim. Chief Brown held up a lantern so Corti could see Garetto's face. "You are the man who shot me," Corti said twice.

At these words, Corti's partner, Novelli, who was also in the wagon, became enraged. He grabbed the lantern and threw it toward Garetto, but it struck Chief Brown in the head instead. Novelli then tried to grab Brown's revolver but was subdued and pulled from the wagon by police.

Despite the efforts of three surgeons, Corti was doomed. The bullet had passed through his stomach and lodged near his spine. He lingered about thirty hours before dying. At his request, he was buried the next day. Hundreds of people attended the service at Hope Cemetery. His

A statue of beloved stone carver Elia Corti adorns his grave in Barre. *Author's photo.*

death stunned the people of Barre and led to a temporary truce between anarchists and socialists.

His brother and brother-in-law carved a remarkable monument to mark his grave. It depicts a dapperly dressed Corti seated with the tools of his trade strewn at his feet. One of his hands rests on a broken column, representing his life cut short. In granite, Corti wears a pensive, perhaps confused look, as if he were trying to figure out what had happened.

In December 1903, Garetto was tried and convicted of manslaughter and sentenced to ten to twelve years of hard labor at Windsor Prison.

Three decades later, as part of the New Deal's Federal Writers' Project, an interviewer asked an old Italian granite worker about his long-dead friend, Elia Corti. The old man remembered learning of Garetto's guilty verdict just before midnight on December 23. Soon afterward, he walked up the street by the Robert Burns Memorial. "It was snowing and not many people were out on the street," he recalled. "When I got close to the statue I saw a man there. It was Corti, plain as day I saw him. Just standing there, his head down a little, and looking at those panels he carved. Sad, he looked, standing there in the snow.

"It seemed natural he was there. I had been thinking all day about him....I wanted to say something but he was gone—just like that! But I saw him. It was Corti all right. And it was one Christmas Eve I can't forget."

25

Silas Griffith's Christmas Gifts

I f Vermont ever had an Ebenezer Scrooge, it was Silas L. Griffith. He was bold, ambitious and often hard-nosed to the point of heartless. Griffith lived to make money, and he was tremendously successful at it. His lumber and charcoal operations eventually employed six hundred people and made him Vermont's first millionaire, back when a million dollars was an even more extraordinary amount of personal wealth than it is today and before there was a permanent federal income tax.

Griffith made his fortune by taking advantage of other people's misfortune; he bought up huge tracts of land, much of it through foreclosure. He eventually amassed fifty thousand acres that sprawled over the towns of Danby, Mount Tabor, Dorset, Arlington, Peru, Manchester, Wallingford and Groton. He had nine sawmills constructed around his vast holdings so that timber had to be hauled only relatively short distances. He had a sawmill built in a part of Mount Tabor that soon became known as Griffith. A small community sprang up around the mill and eventually encompassed forty to fifty structures, including a large boardinghouse for single men, cottages for married men and their families, a blacksmith shop, a harness shop, a wagon shop, a schoolhouse, a general store and stables. Similar communities, though smaller, grew up around the other mills.

Efficiency was the key to Griffith's enterprises. To connect his sprawling empire, Griffith had what are believed to be the first telephone lines in Vermont strung between the main office and each sawmill.

Shrewd—some would say sharp—business practices made Silas Griffith fabulously wealthy. *Mount Tabor–Danby Historical Society.*

Reducing and reusing byproducts and waste was a way to increase profits. He insisted that loggers use saws instead of axes to reduce the amount of wood wasted in felling trees. His sawmills produced great mounds of sawdust, which he sold to icehouses to keep the ice cold.

And he saw great potential in the bits of wood that were too small to be turned into lumber. Griffith hit on the idea of converting the scraps into charcoal. Over time, he had workers build three dozen large brick kilns in clusters at job sites in Danby and Mount Tabor. The kilns stood twenty-five to thirty feet in diameter and rose twelve feet. The kilns converted as much as twenty thousand cords of wood into one million bushels of charcoal annually. The charcoal operations helped feed factories around the Northeast and made Griffith fabulously wealthy.

If Griffith found every way he could to squeeze more money from his land, he did the same with his employees. He refused to let workers wear watches. He didn't want them complaining that they were being overworked. But Griffith insisted that his employees loved their labors. He told a writer for *Outing* magazine in 1885: "[T]hey lead a life of excitement and, to them, one of pleasure. They go to work as early as it is light enough for them to see, and chop until dark."

Griffith's workers were expected to shop for their basic needs at one of the company's six general stores. "By the time they got their work done," says Bradley Bender, president of the Mount Tabor–Danby Historical Society, "they had pretty much paid for their food and clothing."

Loggers and millworkers didn't get rich in Griffith's employ. In fact, some workers fell into debt to him. Bender told of a worker who quit his job at one of the mills. Walking away from the site, he was intercepted by Griffith, who asked the man what he was doing. "Quitting," he replied. Then Griffith reminded the man of his unpaid bills, apparently including the purchase of his pants, which Griffith made the man remove and hand over on the spot.

Arriving in Danby, the reporter for *Outing* magazine watched a worker's coffin being loaded onto a train. The man had been killed when a log rolled onto his chest, crushing him. Griffith chatted with the reporter later that day and eagerly showed off his enterprise. If Griffith had any regrets about the man's death, the reporter didn't mention it.

Griffith was no less sentimental about his first marriage. After twenty-some years of marriage, Elizabeth Staples, who bore Griffith four children, sued for divorce when she learned he had been having an affair with his secretary. When Griffith remarried, this time to the much younger Katherine Tiel, a distant cousin who was a Philadelphia socialite, his new wife refused to live in the house he had shared with Elizabeth. Griffith had the old house torn down and a new one built on the same footprint. He had the lumber from the first house carried to a nearby kiln and converted into charcoal.

All this slashing and burning and profit-making apparently couldn't keep Griffith from wondering whether that was all there was to life. For all his financial success, Griffith suffered a series of personal tragedies. First, his daughter Lottie died at the age of seven weeks. Ten years later, his daughter Agatha died before she turned two. And some years later, his son, Harry, died at age ten, leaving his daughter Jennie as Griffith's lone surviving child.

Like Scrooge—perhaps minus the ghostly visitations—Griffith learned to become more generous. He donated flowers from his greenhouse to local churches and hospitals and provided them for the funerals of townspeople. And before it came his time to die, Griffith made sure to leave a legacy, by financing the construction of a town library. The S.L. Griffith Memorial Library still serves Danby today.

In fact, never one for half measures, Griffith and his wife established a clothing and gift fund in their wills. To this day, the children of Danby and Mount Tabor, ages two to twelve, receive presents courtesy of the Griffiths. Each year shortly before Christmas, children and their families crowd into the Congregational church to watch a yuletide pageant, sing carols and learn a little about Silas Griffith. All the while, children study the pile of presents beneath the large Christmas tree up front. The gifts aren't wrapped, as has apparently always been the tradition. Finally, the children have their names called and they receive their presents, along with a vestige of the nineteenth century—each child also receives candy and an orange, which were rare and expensive treats in Griffith's day and part of the tradition as he envisioned it.

Griffith's business empire is long gone. It closed shortly after his death in 1903. Years of endless cutting had left the hillsides bare; if not for his generosity to the town of Danby and to the area's children, all that would remain today of his work would be some cellar holes, mounds of sawdust and scatterings of bricks. Fortunately, Griffith seems to have realized that there was more to life than money and, like Dickens's character, sought to redeem himself.

26

WOMEN'S BATTLE FOR THE BALLOT

S ocial activism takes the patience of a saint.

Julia Ward Howe, Lucy Stone, Mary Ashton Rice Livermore and William Lloyd Garrison must have known that when they arrived in Vermont in 1870. The renowned reformers were here to fight for one of the most controversial causes of the day: women's right to vote. They believed the time was ripe for change. The Civil War had recently ended, and in its aftermath, black men had been granted the right to vote. Now it was women's turn.

This was a battle to be fought state by state, they believed, not nationally, as black suffrage had been achieved. And Vermont was the place to start. As Lucy Stone's husband and fellow activist, Henry Blackwell, declared, "It is probable that nowhere in the United States can a community be found so well prepared to take this crowning step in political progress." He named several reasons for his confidence, among them that Vermonters "have been reared in the tradition of liberty. No slave ever breathed the elastic air of her hills." He was referring to the fact that Vermont's founders had written a ban on slavery into the state's constitution. (Despite the ban, some slaves had lived in Vermont in its early years.) Blackwell also believed Vermont was fertile ground because about 80 percent of its residents were American-born and therefore not corrupted by foreign influences. He feared that recent immigrants would be less likely to support women's suffrage.

Reformers had reason for hope because of recent successes—and near successes—elsewhere; women's suffrage had just been included in the constitution for the territory of Wyoming, and states like Illinois had come

Lucy Stone, an ardent supporter of women's right to vote, was described as "a modest, quiet, little lady." *Library of Congress.*

close to approving constitutional changes. And in 1870, Vermont was considering just such a change at that year's state constitutional convention.

By nineteenth-century standards, a Vermont woman enjoyed a number of rights that many women elsewhere did not. She could file for divorce on the grounds of adultery, desertion, intolerable severity or nonsupport. Her husband could only sell her property with her permission, and she could will her property to others. Still, once married, her husband became her legal guardian. And she could not vote or hold elected office.

The visiting reformers, all of whom were members of the American Woman Suffrage Association (AWSA), rallied in Vermont to argue for the justice of extending voting rights. Their goal was to convince Vermonters to elect pro-suffrage representatives to the upcoming constitutional convention. The activists may have been celebrities to various extents in their day, but most have largely been forgotten. Ironically, the two best known today, Howe and Garrison, attained fame in other fields—Howe for writing the "Battle Hymn of the Republic" and Garrison for fighting slavery.

The AWSA was a recent creation whose founders wanted to distance themselves from more radical suffrage advocates like Susan B. Anthony and Elizabeth Cady Stanton, who sought more dramatic change, pushing for a national amendment. Stanton had also scandalized some audiences by supporting women's right to divorce and birth control.

Members of the AWSA argued that denying women the vote was subjecting them to taxation without representation. Furthermore, with universal male suffrage now the law of the land, every man—even the ignorant, insane and members of "our foreign population"—could vote, while even the best-qualified woman could not. But the AWSA's goal was too much for some Vermonters. Opponents argued that women were equal within the home and that that was enough, because their husbands represented them in the voting booth. Of course, this argument ignored unmarried women and those who might have voted differently from their husbands.

The activists were trying to appeal to both men and women, but since men were the only ones allowed to vote, they would make the final decision. Indeed, men dominated politics in Vermont to such an extent that when advocates formed the Vermont Woman's Suffrage Association to push for equal voting rights, the organization's founders, and indeed its entire membership, were men.

Newspapers aligned on both sides of the issue. Anti-suffrage papers often focused as much on the hair, clothing and demeanor of the speakers as on the content of their addresses. The *Burlington Free Press* noted the attire of one speaker and complained about her "somewhat singsong, monotonous intonation, and a bad gesture…that looks as though she were trying to nudge somebody." When an Emma Farrand of Fairfield spoke, the paper poked fun at her short hair parted on the side, in the stereotypical style of the "women's rights female"—what we would today call a feminist.

Opponents often worried about the effect politics would have on what was widely seen as the pure nature of women. In contrast, pro-suffrage papers claimed that women would purify politics and had the moral authority to end poverty, crime and intemperance.

The *Montpelier Watchman* was among the newspapers warning that giving women the vote would corrupt them. "Let no woman think she can stand too near the 'dirty pool of politics' and escape the contagion of its foul vapors," the *Watchman* wrote. The paper also declared that "many of [suffrage's] leading advocates…have thrown their scorn and contempt upon the Christian idea of marriage [and]…upon the authority of the Living Word."

During a speech, activist Mary Livermore challenged the *Watchman*'s editor, who was present, to defend that accusation. He chose to remain seated and silent, but from the safety of his office he later attacked Livermore in his paper for her "unwomanly behaviour."

Livermore declared that reading the press accounts, she was "impressed anew with the vulgarity and abuse, the vilification and misrepresentation, the obscene ridicule and ribald jests to which the press of [Vermont] resorts in its opposition to the woman suffrage movement."

The suffragists were not without allies in the press, however. The *Brattleboro Phoenix*, *Green Mountain Freeman* of Montpelier, *Rutland Herald* and *St. Albans Messenger* all supported the drive and reported favorably as the advocates toured the state in the months leading up to the election of delegates to the constitutional convention. A *Herald* reporter wrote that he had expected the reformers to be a bunch of ranting "harpies and Amazons," but upon meeting Lucy Stone, declared her to be "a modest, quiet, little lady of some forty summers." (She was actually fifty-two.)

During the spring of 1870, the reformers barnstormed Vermont in small groups, bringing their message to every corner of the state. Burlington proved particularly inhospitable. Historian Deborah Clifford attributed the city's mood to the strongly anti-suffrage attitude of the local paper. Opponents had derailed a pro-suffrage talk at a church near Burlington by throwing hot pepper on the woodstove, creating a primitive but effective sort of teargas and thereby clearing the room. At another gathering in the city, Julia Ward Howe had a suggestion for her fellow advocates: "Let me come first in the order of exercises," she told them, "as I read from a manuscript and shall not be disconcerted even if they throw chairs at us." Despite fears of violence, the crowd listened quietly.

As the vote for convention delegates loomed, the *Free Press* claimed that an informal poll had found that only 10 percent of Vermont women wanted the right to vote and went so far as to print a petition that it asked women to sign. In part, the petition stated that "we would neglect our family duties"; "prone to excitement, we fear the effects of politics on delicate, pure female character"; and "woman suffrage might lead to laws requiring equal wages for unequal work, since female labor is less skilled."

For all the words that were spoken and printed on the issue, the election of convention delegates that May was something of an anticlimax. The weather on election day was cold and wet; only one in six voters turned out. Those men who did cast ballots were strongly opposed to sharing their right to vote with women.

A month later at the constitutional convention, delegates voted on the proposed amendment without any debate. They defeated the amendment, 231 to 1. Vermont had not proven the fertile ground for change that reformers had hoped. In the end, however, their side would win—it only took another half century to do so.

27

SQUARING OFF OVER MCCARTHYISM

It is hard to imagine Vermont being called soft on anything in 1950, especially by Republicans. The state was as solidly Republican as they came. Members of the GOP had run Vermont ever since the Grand Old Party was formed nearly a century earlier.

But in the early 1950s, the state repeatedly found itself accused of being insufficiently vigilant against the dangers of communism. Critics claimed Vermonters were allowing communist sympathizers and Soviet spies to live, work and—worst yet—teach in the Green Mountain State.

The first accusation came from the national politician after whom the era would be named, U.S. senator Joseph McCarthy of Wisconsin. McCarthy had made headlines in February 1950 when he delivered a stunning speech in which he claimed to possess a list of communist sympathizers and spies embedded in the federal government and in other positions of power. No such list seems to have existed, but McCarthy was off and running.

In July, McCarthy revealed what he claimed to be a plot to pay off the top Soviet spy in the United States under the cover of an innocent-looking land sale in Vermont. The alleged spy was Owen Lattimore, an advisor to the U.S. State Department on Chinese affairs who co-owned a farm in Bethel. Lattimore and other Asia experts were already under investigation for supposedly aiding the Communists' rise to power in China. When those allegations arose, Lattimore had hired a lawyer and racked up enough bills that he had to sell his stake in the farm to pay them. After signing the sales contract, Lattimore learned that the buyer had once run for office as a communist, which is why McCarthy decided to investigate the deal.

McCarthy and other anticommunist crusaders were already suspicious of Vermont. An influential columnist for the Hearst newspaper syndicate claimed that several sympathizers owned vacation homes in the Randolph-Bethel area. In addition, Alger Hiss—a former State Department official recently convicted in connection with allegations that he had spied for the Soviets—summered in Peacham. In announcing his investigation into Lattimore, McCarthy explained that the farm was in the "Hiss area" of Vermont. The *Burlington Free Press* scoffed at implications that the state was rife with communists. "Now that Senator McCarthy has pointed his accusing finger at a land deal in Vermont," the paper editorialized, "perhaps some Vermonters will start looking under their beds at night for lurking Communists." When Lattimore denied under oath that he was a communist sympathizer, he was charged with seven counts of perjury, all of which were eventually dismissed.

In the fall of 1950, Vermont again faced claims that communists were infiltrating the state. This time, the charge came from a veteran Vermont politician, U.S. representative Charles Plumley of Northfield. Having retired months earlier after a seventeen-year career in Congress, Plumley warned that communists and communist sympathizers were working in the state's schools and teaching children with anti-American books. "Nobody doubts that Vermont was selected and that Vermonters were chosen as a bunch of guinea pigs on which to experiment," the seventy-five-year-old politician told a gathering of state Republicans. Plumley called for the establishment of a state censorship board, with members appointed by the governor. Citizens could submit to the board any schoolbook they thought was disloyal to the United States or promoted the interests of a foreign country. If the board ruled the book should be censored, it would contact the local school board, which would be required by law to remove the book from the school. Teachers at a state convention called on Plumley to identify the books he believed must be censored. The former representative declined to name any.

Plumley had trouble rallying Vermonters to his cause. The state's newspapers editorialized against his suggestion. Many Vermonters voiced concerns that a state censorship board would seize control from local communities. But Plumley persuaded a neighbor from Northfield, state representative Charles Barber, to propose a book-censorship law. To promote it, Plumley sought to address the Vermont legislature. When the state senate said it could not hear him before 9:00 p.m. on the date in question, Plumley understood he was being snubbed and refused to speak. When the Vermont House of Representatives finally voted on Barber's censorship bill in March 1953, lawmakers rejected it, 202 to 11.

Left: Retired congressman Charles Plumley of Vermont warned that communists and communist sympathizers were working in the state's schools. *Vermont State Archives*.

Right: U.S. senator Ralph Flanders (R-VT) said that international communism, not exaggerated claims of communist infiltration, was the real threat to the United States. *Library of Congress*.

The lopsided vote didn't mean that some Vermont leaders weren't afraid that communists lurked in their midst, as Alexander Novikoff was about to learn. In April 1953, Novikoff, a cancer researcher at the University of Vermont (UVM), refused to answer questions from the U.S. Senate Subcommittee on Internal Security. The panel wanted to know whether he had been a member of the Communist Party while teaching at Brooklyn College in the late 1930s and early 1940s. UVM president Carl Borgmann came under intense political pressure to fire Novikoff, even though the professor had been granted tenure. Borgmann appointed a six-member committee to review Novikoff's actions and make a recommendation. The committee found that the professor was no longer a communist, if he had ever been one. Noting that he had taken the school's loyalty oath and registered for the military draft, the committee voted five to one to retain Novikoff.

But Governor Lee Emerson, a member of the UVM Board of Trustees, pushed through a motion to suspend Novikoff anyway, withholding his pay and giving him a deadline by which to answer questions. Exasperated, Novikoff's lawyer said, "Dr. Novikoff is charged with the Fifth Amendment." When the deadline arrived, Novikoff maintained his silence, and UVM fired him.

Looking for work, Novikoff got help from America's most prominent scientist, Albert Einstein, who helped him land a job at the just-forming Albert Einstein College of Medicine in New York City, where he became a prominent cancer researcher. Perhaps Einstein was sympathetic because, only two weeks before Novikoff contacted him, McCarthy had labeled Einstein an "enemy of America" for criticizing the anticommunist hunt.

The real threat to the country, argued U.S. senator Ralph Flanders of Vermont, was McCarthy himself. Flanders agreed with McCarthy that communism posed a danger to America, but it was international communism led by Russia and China that worried Flanders, not exaggerated claims of communist infiltration in this country. To Flanders, McCarthy's tactics were a distraction from greater threats.

"[W]e are being diverted, and to an extent dangerous to our future as a nation," said Flanders in a speech in March 1954. He saw the Iron Curtain of communism advancing in Korea and Indochina and communists gaining power in Europe. Flanders feared he was witnessing a recurrence of the fall of nations at the start of World War II.

The speech received muted praise. President Dwight Eisenhower sent a two-sentence note thanking Flanders for his comments. Flanders's words had no effect on McCarthy, who continued his crusade. For two months in the spring of 1954, the senator conducted what became known as the Army-McCarthy hearings, claiming that the army was rife with communists. The spectacle was broadcast live to the nation, giving Americans their first view of McCarthy's bullying tactics. Most Vermonters relied on newspaper and radio accounts, because the state's first television transmitter would not be erected until that fall.

McCarthy's performance outraged Flanders, who called on the Senate to remove the senator from his controversial committee. When the Republican Senate leader buried Flanders's resolution in committee, Flanders filed a second resolution in late July, this time calling for senators to censure McCarthy for his conduct. With an election looming, Republican Senate leaders managed to delay the vote. Finally, a month after the election, senators voted sixty-seven to twenty-two to censure McCarthy. Flanders and George Aiken, Vermont's other Republican senator, joined twenty Republicans and forty-five Democrats in voting against McCarthy.

A legislative rebuke might seem an unlikely way to stop a political heavyweight like McCarthy, but it did the trick. After the censure vote, senators suddenly felt free to take on the senator—or to ignore him. Thanks to a resolution pushed by a Vermont senator, President Eisenhower was able to joke with his cabinet that McCarthyism had just become "McCarthywasm."

PART V
RIDING WAVES OF CHANGE

28

Arrival of Cars Spells Doom for Some

The future arrived in Vermont in 1898.

Burlington residents watched in wonder as Dr. Joseph H. Linsley putted around in his new Stanley Steamer, which is believed to be the first automobile ever driven in Vermont. That didn't mean the state didn't already have a law on the books governing motor vehicles. Vermonters may be a law-abiding people, but they are also a law-writing people. Passed four years before Dr. Linsley bought his car from the Stanley Brothers of Massachusetts, the law required that anyone "in charge of a carriage, vehicle or engine propelled by steam" shall not drive on a public road without having a person "of mature age" walking at least one-eighth of a mile ahead to warn people that a motor car was approaching. At night, this person was to carry a red light.

In a sense, those people walking ahead with their lights might have been warning Vermont how much automobiles were going to change the state. Vermonters seemed both enthralled with and concerned by these new contraptions. Some worked to promote cars, while other Vermonters dedicated themselves to regulate or ban them outright.

Dr. Horatio Nelson Jackson was among the promoters. In a well-publicized stunt, Jackson became the first person to drive cross-country by car, taking sixty-three days to travel from San Francisco to New York. The going was never easy. Though the United States had more than 2,000,000 miles of roads at the time, only 150 of those miles were paved. Jackson figured the trip set him back $8,000, factoring in the cost of the car, the salary of the driver-mechanic who accompanied him, the expense of gas and the cost

Vermont's deeply rutted, muddy roads have always been the bane of automobiles. *Vermont State Archives.*

of multiple repairs along the way. Add to that $6—the cost of the fine he received for speeding when he returned to his hometown of Burlington after the journey. He'd been caught exceeding the six-mile-per-hour speed limit.

That was quite fast enough, the Vermont legislature had recently decided when it set statewide speed limits. Six miles per hour was the limit in village, town and city centers. Outside of settled areas, drivers were welcome to hit fifteen miles per hour. Those conservative limits probably made sense. Think of the realities of the time: horses were ubiquitous and didn't mix well with fast cars; pedestrians were unfamiliar with how to interact with cars; the skills of new drivers, which at the time would have been everyone, were probably weak; early automobiles had abysmal safety records; and road conditions were poor at best. To have some oversight over automobiles, the legislature started requiring drivers to register their vehicles in 1904. Motor vehicles were still luxury items; in 1906, only 373 had been registered in Vermont.

To prominent Vermonter Joseph Battell, however, that was exactly 373 too many. "Let the owners of the highway dragons build their own roads," snarled Battell. Thanks to a large inheritance, Battell was rich and powerful. He also had a thing for horses. Battell had purchased a five-hundred-acre farm in Weybridge for the selective breeding of a horse breed long associated with Vermont, the Morgan. Battell's love of horses is probably what fueled his hatred of automobiles. "It is impossible that highways can be used with safety and comfort by the two methods of travel," he declared.

Wealthy Vermonter Joseph Battell tried to ban cars from driving past his inn. When that failed, he scattered debris on the road. *Library of Congress.*

Battell fought against automobiles in several ways. As a state legislator, he introduced a bill to ban motor traffic on the Hancock-Ripton Road, which, not coincidentally, ran past an inn he owned in Ripton. When the bill failed, Battell attacked the issue less like a sage lawmaker and more like a vindictive neighbor. He took to erecting barriers and spreading debris in the road near his inn. When the legislature learned of his actions, it criminalized such behavior. Battell had still another way to fight this new invasive species. He owned a newspaper, the *Middlebury Register*, and he started filling its pages with reprinted stories about car crashes, especially those involving women and children.

Battell certainly would have known of the incident that occurred on August 14, 1905. That day, Harris Lindsley had the unfortunate distinction of making history on the roads of Vermont. Lindsley, who was the deputy police commissioner of New York City, was touring Vermont with his fiancée, Evelyn Pierpont Willing, an heiress from a well-known Chicago family. Willing, whose late mother had Vermont roots, had taken to summering at the Equinox in Manchester. She was there in 1905 with some family members, including an aunt and nephew. Some people later said that the couple was to be married the following week.

That August day, the couple was heading south to Williamstown, Massachusetts. They rode in the backseat of a large automobile, a "big touring machine," as one newspaper account described it, with brass Chicago plates—the state of Illinois hadn't yet started issuing plates. Up front were Willing's nephew, Ambrose Cramer, and the chauffeur, J.A. Adamson.

As the car approached Pike's Crossing, a railroad crossing just north of Bennington, Adamson accelerated the vehicle because of the incline, hitting an estimated twenty miles per hour. If he glimpsed the approaching train, he might have hit the gas harder. The front of the car cleared the tracks before the train struck, so the back seat bore the brunt of the impact. The collision threw the automobile about fifty feet. The train, which consisted of only a locomotive and a passenger car, derailed. The train cars rolled over and came to a rest about ten or fifteen feet from the tracks, about one hundred feet of which were torn up by the collision. The engineer and fireman jumped to safety, and the train's fifteen passengers were not seriously injured.

But the impact crushed the car, which caught fire. Miraculously, Adamson and Cramer survived the crash with only some bad cuts and bruises. Lindsley and Willing weren't so lucky. They became the first people killed in an automobile accident in Vermont. A subsequent investigation found that the train had been driving backward—that is, with the engine in the rear—at the time of the crash. The position of the engineer blocked his view of the approaching car. A state railroad committee, however, laid most of the blame on Adamson for not stopping at the crossing, not seeing or hearing the train and for speeding.

After the accident, the bodies of Lindsley and Willing lay in state at the Mark Skinner Library in Manchester so members of the public could pay their respects. It might seem an odd use for a library, but Willing was Skinner's granddaughter, and her mother had donated the library to the town. Willing was then buried in Manchester's Dellwood Cemetery, and a train transported Lindsley's body south to Grand Central Station in New York, where it was met by a crowd. Military and police officers, twenty-five mounted and forty others on foot, escorted the casket to a military armory, where his body lay in state. The next day, the casket was taken back to Grand Central Station for the long ride back to Vermont. Lindsley was buried beside his fiancée.

Joseph Battell would certainly have argued that the lovers' fates were a stern reminder of the dangers posed by automobiles. Of course, it was an argument he would lose.

29

MISSING THE CHANCE
TO GIVE WOMEN THE VOTE

Vermont had a date with history. The Nineteenth Amendment, the one giving women the right to vote in all elections, had been ratified by thirty-five state legislatures. Vermont hadn't yet weighed in on the matter. If it passed the amendment, the state could claim credit for casting the deciding vote making it the law of the land.

But a major obstacle stood in the way: Vermont governor Percival Clement. The governor opposed women's suffrage on political grounds. He was afraid how they would vote. And from his political perspective, he had good reason. If women got the vote, he would lose a fight he had long been waging. Clement knew that women voters were likely to overwhelmingly support prohibition. In recent decades, women had made inroads into political life by focusing on "issues of the hearth," matters that affected children or the family. Prohibition was their principal cause.

Clement hated the idea of the federal government telling states to ban alcoholic beverages. He favored local control—very local control. Clement was an advocate of what was called local option. He believed every city and town had the right to decide whether it wanted to be "wet" or "dry."

Clement opposed prohibition from the start of his statewide political career. He had represented Rutland in the Vermont House in 1892 and served two terms as Rutland's mayor when he decided to run for governor. His campaign in 1902 was a challenge to Republican Party leaders. The Proctors, a family that had gotten rich in the marble industry, largely controlled who got nominated to the Republican ticket. In those days, when the Democrats were a weak party, that was as good as getting elected. "The time has come when we have got to purify the Republican Party from the damnable machine which has been on top of it," Clement declared.

But Clement was hardly an anti-establishment candidate. He came to the campaign with tremendous wealth. The son of a marble magnate himself, Clement owned the *Rutland Herald* newspaper, the Rutland Railroad, several hotels, a bank and a brokerage firm. His challenge to the Proctors was partly a contest between families for dominance in Rutland and Vermont.

Clement used his railroad to his advantage, riding it to communities around the state as he stumped. In his speeches, Clement promoted the idea of a local option law and attacked prohibition as an infringement of

Governor Percival Clement opposed ratification of the Nineteenth Amendment because he feared women voters would back a national ban on alcohol. *Wikimedia Commons*.

personal rights. He drew large, supportive crowds, but the Proctors won out when, at the party convention, their handpicked candidate, John McCullough, was elected on the third ballot.

Clement continued the fight, setting up a third party, the Local Option League, so he could run in that fall's election. He ended up losing but managed to win 40 percent of the vote and keep McCullough below 50 percent—the first time a Republican statewide candidate had been denied a majority since the party took control of Vermont politics in the 1850s. Since no candidate had won a majority, by law it fell to the legislature to decide the winner. The legislature picked McCullough.

Though he lost the election, Clement won on his main issue. His challenge had threatened the Republican leadership. To weaken Clement's insurgency, the Republican-controlled legislature moved quickly to enact a local option law. The legislation, if passed, would be a bold action, since it would end the state's fifty years of prohibition. So lawmakers, looking for political cover on this divisive issue, put the matter up for a public referendum. State law does not allow for binding referenda, but the legislature found a way around that. The referendum asked voters to pick which date the new law would take effect. If voters picked the later date, it was understood that lawmakers would preserve statewide prohibition. Vermonters picked the earlier date. Local option found most of its support in the state's largest communities, which were trying to compete for tourists with vacation areas in other states that did not prohibit alcohol.

In 1906, Clement again challenged the Republican hierarchy, but with local option gone as an issue, he was roundly defeated. This time he lost to a Proctor. Clement ran as a Democrat and received only 38 percent of the vote compared with 60 percent for Fletcher Proctor, son of former governor Redfield Proctor. Having perhaps learned his lesson, Clement returned to the Republican Party and won election as Rutland mayor in 1911 and 1912. By 1918, Clement was again ready to run for governor. In the Republican primary, he edged out three challengers, winning a mere 37 percent of the vote. In the general election, voters, most of them Republicans, forgave him for his dalliance with the Democrats and rewarded him with 67 percent of the vote.

Clement had finally reached the governor's office. When he arrived, the issue of prohibition had returned. This time, it was a national matter. Congress had approved a constitutional amendment in December 1917 banning alcoholic beverages. Now it was up to the legislatures of the states to approve or reject it. The Vermont legislature brought it up for a vote in January 1919, just as Clement was reaching office.

Popular opinion was divided on the matter. A referendum in 1916 suggesting a return to statewide prohibition was defeated. But only thirteen communities had taken advantage of the local option to declare themselves wet. The state legislature ended up supporting the Eighteenth Amendment, approving prohibition on January 26, 1919. But the vote was largely symbolic, coming as it did two weeks after the amendment had been approved by enough state legislatures to win national ratification.

During the same legislative session, Vermont lawmakers approved granting women the right to vote in presidential elections—women here had already won the right to vote in school elections and, if they were taxpayers, also in municipal elections. All that the bill needed to become law was Clement's signature. But he refused to give it. Instead, he vetoed the bill; the legislature couldn't muster the votes to override his veto.

In June 1919, Congress sent the Nineteenth Amendment, guaranteeing women the right to vote, to the states for ratification. By April 1920, the amendment needed approval from just one more state to be ratified.

Suffragettes protest against Republican opposition in Vermont and other states to women's right to vote. *Wikimedia Commons.*

Supporters lobbied Clement to call a special session. If he acted quickly, Vermont would win the honor of putting the amendment over the top. But he wouldn't be moved. Clement apparently believed that allowing women the vote would make it impossible to repeal prohibition.

Clement's Republican lieutenant governor, Mason Stone, publicly supported the amendment. Stone's position made Clement a virtual prisoner. The governor believed that if he traveled outside the state, Stone, as acting governor, would convene a special session. The national Republican Party supported the amendment. Perhaps to ease its passage, it notified Clement that he was needed in Washington to help devise a presidential campaign strategy for Warren Harding. Clement was torn. He wanted to go. The summons was an honor and a responsibility. So he struck a deal with Stone in which he could leave the state without the lieutenant governor calling a special session, unless he failed to return by a set date. What Stone got out of the bargain is unknown. Clement went to Washington and returned in time to forestall a special session.

Vermont's legislature finally approved the Nineteenth Amendment on February 8, 1921, during its regular session. The approval was just a formality. It came *after* Vermont women had voted in their first presidential election. Six months earlier, the chance to cast the deciding vote for national ratification had been seized by Tennessee.

30

THE HORROR OF THE SPANISH INFLUENZA

D r. Charles Dalton must have felt helpless. He saw disaster coming but could do nothing to stop it. The dreaded Spanish influenza that had ravaged Europe in the summer and fall of 1918 was about to strike Vermont. As secretary of the Vermont State Board of Health, Dalton could do little more than chart its progress as the disease tore through the state. On September 21, he ordered local health officers to report any influenza cases. Three days later, the state's newspapers issued his warning that the epidemic would reach Vermont in the coming days or weeks.

Even that prediction proved too optimistic. The disease was already here. The *Rutland Herald* reported that day that 40 students at Middlebury College were sick and 60 at Norwich University. They were among the first of perhaps 50,000 Vermonters who would be stricken. More than 1,800 would die.

The world was facing one of its worst epidemics ever. In little over a year, the disease would kill between twenty million and fifty million people worldwide, nearly half of them in India. The Black Death, which ebbed and flowed in medieval Europe, killed as many as forty million people—but it took 150 years to do so.

The Spanish influenza epidemic still haunts epidemiologists. It killed so many by being highly contagious; in the days before global air travel, the disease managed to span the world.

Dalton didn't underestimate the danger posed by the virus. "The disease itself is not serious; the complications frequently are," he wrote. "Hence, the disease should not be slighted." Many who died in the epidemic were killed by pneumonia brought on by the influenza.

Governor Horace Graham, at home in Craftsbury, was disturbed by the newspaper reports he'd been reading. He wrote Dalton on September 26: "Do you not think some general action ought to be taken by the Board [of Health] with reference to this epidemic[?] If it is contagious what about permitting all these conventions and meetings[?]" But Graham also worried about the effect that banning gatherings would have on the sale of Liberty Bonds to fund World War I, then raging in Europe.

The next day, Dalton issued an order to local health officers. While the state probably would not close schools, churches or other places of public assembly, he wrote, health officers should know they have the right to do so. "Health officers," he continued, "should make it plain to all persons that the disease is spread by coughing and sneezing in public or around other people." Funerals for flu victims were allowed, Dalton said, but anyone who had been in contact with the sick was barred from attending.

Dalton knew the flu killed quickly. By the end of September, Vermonters were dying in waves. In the hardest-hit community, Barre, ten people died over the weekend of September 28 and 29. Twelve more died on September 30 and the morning of October 1. The next day, seventeen more died.

"Undertakers, between ambulance calls and more serious missions, are having little time for sleep," reported the *Barre Daily Times* in an era when funeral homes often ran the local ambulance service. Front-page obituaries, briefly outlining the lives and deaths of a baker, a policeman, a housewife, a stonecutter, began crowding out news from the battlefields of Europe. The paper's social notes, usually filled with banter about who was visiting whom, now reported who was ill.

Life was easier in the southern half of the state. Still, Brattleboro had sixty-five reported flu cases, including a family of seven that was rushed to the hospital. Middlebury College banned students from leaving campus and turned the second floor of Hepburn Hall into an influenza ward.

Elsewhere, other institutions began taking what precautions they could to halt the disease's progress. St. Johnsbury banned public meetings. With half the students out sick in some grades, Barre closed its schools, as did Montpelier and Wells River. The state supreme court postponed the start of its session. Many sections of Vermont pleaded for more doctors. The University of Vermont sent medical students on a special train to Barre. Rutland's call for nurses went largely unheeded. Medical personnel went where the need was greatest.

The University of Vermont gymnasium, converted to a medical clinic, awaits the arrival of patients during the Spanish influenza epidemic of 1918. *University of Vermont Special Collections.*

Vermont was not alone in the crisis. In late September, Massachusetts's lieutenant governor, Calvin Coolidge, a Vermont native, wired surrounding states, asking for doctors to treat the ailing in his state. Governor Graham responded that Vermont could spare none. Nationwide, one-quarter of the country's doctors and one-third of its nurses were serving in the military.

On October 4, Dalton took the step he thought would be unnecessary: he ordered all of the state's schools, churches and theaters closed and prohibited all public gatherings. He had good reason. By the end of the first week of October, Barre was reporting 2,000 influenza cases. St. Johnsbury had 842 cases, St. Albans 750 and Montpelier 500. In contrast, to the south, Rutland City had 146 cases, Proctor 169, Brattleboro 86 and Manchester only 10. Springfield and Hartford were the only hard-hit towns in the state's southern half, with 692 and 584 cases, respectively.

The flu was now claiming more victims than the war. Between September 1 and October 7, the *Barre Daily Times* noted, fifteen Vermonters serving in the military were killed in action, but thirty-seven others died of pneumonia after contracting the flu.

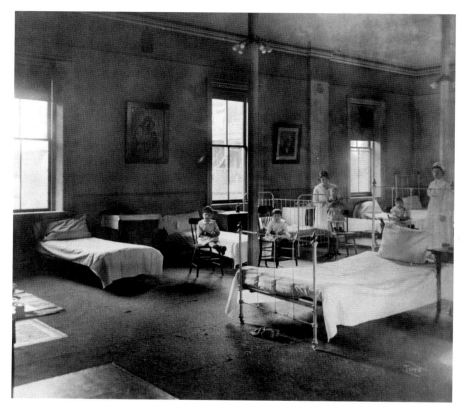

Children whose parents fell ill during the Spanish influenza epidemic are cared for at the First Congregational Church in Burlington. *Vermont Historical Society.*

The epidemic devastated families. A father and son in the Pombrio family of Barre died on October 4. The mother died on October 6, and her seventeen-year-old son followed her to the grave four days later, leaving three brothers and sisters to fend for themselves.

By mid-October, the epidemic had peaked. On October 14, readers of the *Rutland Herald* must have been relieved to see headlines promising better times. "Brattleboro on the Mend," one announced; another read, "Montpelier Continues to Improve." All told, Barre would lose 177 residents to the epidemic. But by October 15, the *Barre Daily Times* could declare, "Barre no longer lies supine in the grasp of influenza and pneumonia, as decreasing death lists and rapidly increasing recovery totals plainly indicate."

The worst was over. On October 31, Dalton lifted his ban on public gatherings. With his new order, Dalton also helped lift the pall that had shrouded daily life.

Most Vermonters probably knew someone who had died. The epidemic had killed one out of every two hundred Vermonters.

Gifford Owen was one of the survivors. As a ten-year-old living in Montgomery Center at the time, Owen and seven family members had contracted the disease. One of his sisters managed to stay healthy. Her reward was that she got to care for the others. Years later, Owen recalled the day he was allowed to leave his sickbed and walk several blocks on an errand. Recent rains had turned the roads muddy, but the day's cold weather had formed a crust over them. "Horses' hooves left hundreds and hundreds of mirror-like holes in the road," he said. "Breaking those little ponds was such a delight. Even the air was different. I remember breathing real hard to inhale something I hadn't felt in weeks....And the wonderment of being able to walk, it's as if you had come back from the grave."

31

SEEKING THE GOOD LIFE IN VERMONT

It was a radical step, one that would be nearly as radical today as it was when Helen and Scott Nearing took it in the early 1930s. Disgusted by what they saw as an immoral society based on war, greed and unearned income, the Nearings decided to leave that world behind. They would create their own world here in Vermont, this one based on the freedom of the subsistence farmer, cooperation with neighbors and bartered transactions instead of financial ones whenever possible. Their Vermont experiment lasted two decades before they picked up stakes and moved to Maine to continue the project for another three decades. Their successes inspired a new generation that would attempt to leave aspects of the larger world behind by moving back to the land.

The Nearings were unlikely radicals. Both were born into money. Scott grew up as one of the few privileged people in the company town of Morris Run, Pennsylvania. His grandfather ran the company that owned the local coal mines and forests, as well as the stores, churches and schools. Nearing remembered that, when he was about five, he watched a worker pick up a twenty-foot length of half-inch chain and carry it slowly toward a car he was loading. "Why don't the guy do that faster?" he thought. "Why don't he hurry?" When he tried to lift the chain himself, Nearing understood. "That was one of my first lessons," he told historian Studs Terkel. "The people who work have to move chains and split wood and do all the other things that require energy, determination, and a whole lot of juice. The other people lie in hammocks." The sense of class-consciousness that awakened in Nearing that day stayed with him for the remaining ninety-five years of his life. He would turn his back on the system that had enriched his family.

Nearing studied economics and then taught it at the University of Pennsylvania, often attacking the capitalist system as unfair and immoral. When in 1915 he promoted a bill in the state legislature banning child labor, an influential textile mill owner threatened to use his connections to cut the school's state funding unless Nearing was fired. The administration acquiesced and sacked him. Two years later, Nearing was in trouble again, this time with the federal government for writing a tract opposing the Great War, which was then raging. The government was trying to quash dissent. Nearing lost on appeal to the U.S. Supreme Court and had to pay $3,000 for airing his views. "It was a vocal country," Nearing told Terkel. "The First World War ended it."

Helen Knothe also grew up in comfort, but her childhood home was freer than Scott's. Helen's mother was a Dutch artist who encouraged her daughter to travel widely and explore life. As a young woman, Helen responded by following Krishnamurti, the Indian spiritual leader who counseled self-awareness. Helen was only twenty-four years old when she met Scott Nearing, who was forty-five and separated from his first wife. The two hit it off. Soon, Helen wanted to live with Scott, but he suggested she take a sort of test to see if she was ready to surrender her privileged life. First, Helen took a job at a candy factory in Brooklyn and lived in a nearby slum. When she asked for a raise, she was fired. Then she traveled to Europe in luxury, to see if she missed the trappings of wealth. When she decided she

The experiences of Scott and Helen Nearing helped trigger the back-to-the-land movement in Vermont. *Library of Congress.*

didn't, Helen sailed back to the United States and set up house with Scott in a cold-water flat in New York City. There, they forsook their families' wealth and lived on what money they earned.

In 1932, with the nation in the midst of the Great Depression, the Nearings decided to move to New England, where they thought they could live more independently. They picked Vermont, the Nearings later wrote, because they "liked the thickly forested hills which formed the Green Mountains. The valleys were cosy, the people unpretentious." The Nearings put $300 down on a rundown farm that included land in Stratton, Winhall and Jamaica. They put in their own garden, which grew about 80 percent of the food they needed. As vegetarians, they raised no animals. They cut their own wood and constructed buildings out of stones they pulled from the land. They used pretty much everything they produced. Their only cash crop was maple syrup and maple sugar, which they traded with friends down south for citrus fruit and other goods they couldn't produce themselves.

As much as they could, they avoided participating in the money economy. Their main need for cash was to pay their property taxes. "We were poor in the country, but it was better than being poor in the city," Helen told Terkel. "Instead of eating out of garbage cans, we ate out of our own garden. It was quite novel for me. My family had a garden and a gardener."

Scott spoke of Vermont, and later of Maine, as their "cyclone cellar in New England," which provided shelter from what in their view was the immoral world beyond. But, he insisted, they were not escapists: "[W]e were not shirking obligations, but looking for an opportunity to take on more worthwhile experiences."

Since the Nearings never sought to make a profit, they worked only as hard as they had to on the farm. Typically, they divided their days into three blocks of four hours each. They spent one of the blocks performing "bread labor," the work necessary to provide their necessities—food, shelter and clothing. They devoted another block to personal pursuits—writing, playing music, skiing. The final block was left for civic work, which entailed doing something of value for the community, such as helping a neighbor or entertaining visitors.

As the Nearings' fame grew, so did the number of visitors. Eventually, the couple posted a sign at the end of their driveway informing would-be guests that they only welcomed folks during certain hours or if they called ahead. What drew people to their farm was that the Nearings had succeeded in showing that they could live by their own labor, almost entirely outside the capitalist system. They wanted to exemplify the type of independent life that was possible if one had the courage to leave mainstream life behind. Beginning in the 1960s, they served as role models for back-to-the-landers who sought a simpler, better life in Vermont.

But they wouldn't be here to witness that period. They had had a loftier goal than just self-sufficiency when they moved north. They had wanted to show the benefits of cooperation. Occasionally, a neighbor or two might work with them during maple sugaring season, or some idealistic city dwellers might work with them for a while, but the Nearings' vision of a dynamic communal life never materialized. In dissecting their failure in their now-famous book *Living the Good Life: How to Live Sanely and Simply in a Troubled World*, they wrote, "In one sense Vermont offered less rather than more opportunity for collective experiments than most other parts of rural America. Vermonters were strong individualists…and all the major Vermont traditions emphasized the individualism of the Green Mountain folk."

Vermonters, the Nearings believed, worked together better as families than as communities. Their neighbors were organized into "autonomous households," they wrote. In fact, "'Autonomous' is hardly the word," they continued. "'Sovereign' would be a more exact descriptive term."

The Nearings abandoned their idea of a more communal life and moved to Maine in 1952. By then, the couple's farm had grown to 750 acres. With the development of a ski area at Stratton Mountain, the land's value had skyrocketed from about $2.75 an acre to $8,000. Land they had purchased for about $2,000 was now worth $6,000,000 on the market. But they couldn't accept the fortune they would have made by selling it. "We had done nothing to justify the increase," Scott explained. So they decided to donate the land to the town for a municipal forest.

It was then, perhaps, that the Nearings understood the extent of the distrust their radical ideas had engendered in the town. When residents considered whether to accept this gift at the next town meeting, one-third of them voted "no." "The Korean War was on at the time," Scott said. "Those opposed to acceptance called us Communists. They thought we were trying to bribe the town in some way."

Despite the suspicions people harbored about them, the Nearings made it clear that it was more the arrival of skiers, the leisure class, that drove them away. "We wanted to live with people who earned their living by ordinary means instead of artificialities," Scott said. "We liked the farmers better."

32

They Saw Gold in White Slopes

Lumberman Craig Burt knew he was risking ridicule by even writing the letter. But he was convinced he was right. The year was 1935, and Burt thought he had a way for Vermont businesses to make a little more money. "I know that to some, statements which I have made will seem visionary and unsound," he wrote in a letter to the editor of the *Bennington Banner* newspaper. Burt's peculiar idea was that the state should promote the new sport of downhill skiing. "[T]o one who has been interested for a decade, and has met and talked with those who have investigated Europe, it is just as sure and as good-business as any summer development we have, and much better than some."

As co-owner of the C.E. & F.O. Burt Lumber Company of Stowe, Burt owned a large chunk of land on Mount Mansfield. The area had been a resort for nearly eighty years when he wrote his letter. A luxurious hotel had been built just below the summit in 1858, but it catered only to the summer set.

Skiing was little known in the valley well into the twentieth century. The first skiers in the area may have been members of several Swedish families who moved there in 1912. Burt was intrigued. Like the Swedes, he viewed skiing as a form of transportation more than recreation. He bought a pair of skis and used them to tour his property and to make the occasional jaunt up the mountain.

But in 1921, with the town in an economic slump, Burt suggested a winter carnival that would include skating, a toboggan run and other winter games, including ski jumping. That first festival did spawn an annual tradition that continues today, but it did not make the town a skiing mecca. The events that would make Stowe the "ski capital of the East" would occur a decade later.

In 1930, at the suggestion of a friend, Burt began opening his logging company's Ranch Camp to skiers. Only the most diehard took Burt up on his offer. These were the days before ski lifts or rope tows. The only way uphill was on foot or ski.

It was just as well that the slopes would accommodate only serious skiers, since the town's inns and guesthouses at the time boasted only about sixty beds. The nation was in the midst of the Great Depression, and Stowe was a fairly sleepy town even in normal times. It was hardly a propitious moment to launch a new industry, one might think, but Stowe's timing couldn't have been better. In 1933, Congress created the federally funded Civilian Conservation Corps, a massive public works program that put millions to work on such projects as building roads and dams, renovating old buildings and stringing phone lines. When a group of CCC workers was dispatched to Vermont, it was up to State Forester Perry Merrill to decide what tasks to assign them. At the suggestion of a member of the local Stowe Ski Club, Merrill arranged for a squad to cut ski trails on Mount Mansfield. This investment of public money helped establish the

The opening of a ski area on Mount Mansfield attracted swarms of visitors to the once sleepy town of Stowe. *Vermont State Archives.*

idea that ski development was for the public good, since it would bring tourists into the state. Later in the 1930s, ski area owners began to expect the state to upgrade roads leading to their slopes and make them passable quickly after snowstorms. (These attempts to get government assistance for the ski industry pale compared to the effort Walter Schoenknecht, founder of Mount Snow, made in 1963, when he petitioned the Atomic Energy Commission to have an atomic bomb detonated at his mountain to create a ski bowl. The commission declined the suggestion.)

All the government help imaginable wasn't going to make skiing popular if it couldn't overcome the main barrier: the sport was simply too strenuous for all but the diehard. Since skiers had to spend most of their time climbing uphill, not skiing down, even fit skiers might only manage a handful of runs in a day. It was clear that if the sport was to draw more skiers to areas around the state, a technological innovation would be needed.

One evening in January 1934, a group of skiers, gathered at the White Cupboard Inn in Woodstock, were bemoaning the arduous climbs they had had to make that day. As the skiers, young businessmen from New York City, sat complaining about their sore muscles, they hit upon an idea. "[E]ach of us is spending $40 apiece to enjoy a weekend in Vermont," one of the men told the innkeepers, "yet the most we can do in a day is to climb a hill half a dozen times. We want to get in all the skiing we can on a weekend. We want to be carried uphill."

The businessmen pledged at least seventy-five dollars to the inn's owners, Robert and Elizabeth Royce, if they could come up with a way to create a more favorable ratio of downhill exhilaration to uphill drudgery. The skiers said they would be back in mid-February and asked the Royces to have something in place by then.

Despite the short deadline, the Royces succeeded. They tracked down a rumor that a ski club in Quebec had such a device—not an easy task in the days before the Internet. Using a crude diagram provided by the club, a couple of talented mechanics hired by the Royces set to work. The main parts were eighteen hundred feet of rope, some pulleys and an old Model T Ford truck to power it. The result was the first towrope in America. The total cost came to $500, which the skiers gratefully paid. The Royces had the tow set up on a sloping pasture they leased from local farmer Clinton Gilbert. Towropes transformed skiing from a sport open only to the most physically fit to one that almost anyone could try.

The Royces' tow had an equally startling effect on Woodstock. Suddenly, the town became a skiing mecca. Ever since the Woodstock Inn opened in

Vermont's ski industry began to grow steadily in the 1940s. *Vermont State Archives*.

1892, the town had been a fashionable destination for outdoor recreation. But this was something different.

"The hundreds and hundreds of skiers who thronged the streets on Saturday nights, overflowed the eating-places, and startled housewives with requests for beds, bewildered the sober citizenry," wrote Charles Crane in the 1940s in his book *Winter in Vermont*. "Every third house along the main roads hung out its 'Skiers Accommodated' sign, winter-idle youths took to taxi-driving, and new tows were quickly constructed to meet the overwhelming demand."

Railroads, seeing great potential in the ski traffic, began running more trains to the ski areas that were popping up across Vermont. In the mid-1930s, Woodstock had plenty of company. Soon, seemingly every town with steep, open fields and access to good roads or a train station had its own ski area. A state report in 1938 listed thirty-three communities offering skiing. Many of them, including Barre City, Barton, Brandon, Fair Haven and Shrewsbury, have left their skiing days far behind. Others on that list, towns like Sherburne (now Killington), Cambridge and Stowe, remain mainstays in Vermont's ski industry.

When Mount Mansfield installed its own towrope in 1936, skiers could ride it only partway up the mountain. They had to hike higher if they wanted to try the more challenging terrain near the peak. A group of investors, including famed outdoorsman Lowell Thomas, backed plans to install a chairlift that would carry skiers nearly to the summit. The lift, which opened in late 1940, cost the company the staggering figure of $100,000. Skiers paid about $1 per ride, compared with Woodstock's towrope service, which initially charged $1 a day. The company took in only $3,840 in gross revenues that first season. Word must have gotten out, however, as revenues for 1941 soared to more than $31,000, even though the country had just entered World War II.

When the war ended, Stowe was ready to boom. During the winter of 1946–47, more than 105,000 skiers rode the resort's lifts. The town grew to meet the ballooning demand. Whereas in the early 1930s the town could offer only about sixty beds, by 1951, developers had built enough inns, hotels and motels in Stowe to accommodate 14,000 skiers a night.

By then, those skiers, and the money they brought into the state, were a major revenue source for Vermont's economy. Nobody thought of Craig Burt and other early ski promoters as anything but right.

33

The Beginning of the End
for Small Dairy Farms

Tipping points in history aren't always the sudden, dramatic events we might imagine. It doesn't take the rise and fall of leaders, the outbreak of war or a natural disaster to change the course of history. Sometimes, the tipping point can be something seemingly mundane. Vermont experienced such a change in the mid-1900s, when, to cut their costs, companies began promoting a simple new technology that ended up transforming the state's rural economy and landscape.

The Vermont of the early 1950s was markedly different from the state we know today. In 1953, Vermont boasted nearly eleven thousand dairy farms, which formed the backbone of the state's rural communities. The state could accommodate so many farms because most were small family operations. The average Vermont herd had only twenty-five milking cows. But by 1963, one-third of those farms had closed. By 1970, the number had been cut by nearly two-thirds. And today, the state is home to fewer than one thousand dairy farms—less than 10 percent of the total it had in 1953.

Over the years, a variety of factors contributed to this precipitous decline, but the one that started the plunge was the mandated adoption of a machine to chill large quantities of milk on farms. Beginning in 1952, milk handlers from Massachusetts and Vermont began pushing farmers to install stainless steel bulk tanks. The tanks made it easier for the handlers to collect milk, thereby cutting their expenses. The cost of the shiny new tanks, however, was borne by farmers—or, in thousands of instances, *not* borne by farmers, who instead decided to go out of business because the investment was too expensive.

The move to bulk tanks didn't happen in isolation. Until the late 1800s, Vermont's numerous local dairy cooperatives and factories processed much of the state's milk supply into butter and cheese, since less-perishable products could be shipped to distant markets. But the dairy industry changed in 1890, when the first rail shipments of Vermont milk left Bellows Falls, headed for Boston. Railroads, and the advent of refrigerated rail cars, gave Vermont dairy farmers access to the Northeast's growing market for fluid milk. The arrangement tied them to an increasingly competitive market.

So it was that, starting in the 1950s, when milk handlers saw that bulk tanks could reduce their costs, they urged and eventually required farmers to use them. This was solely an industry mandate. The state government's only involvement was issuing and enforcing sanitary regulations regarding the tanks.

Before bulk tanks, farmers had stored milk in ten-gallon metal cans. The process was labor intensive. Farmers would milk either by hand or by machine into milk pails. They would then carry the pails to the milk house, usually attached to the barn, where they would pour the milk through a strainer into the cans. Once a can was full, the farmer would put it into a cooler. If the farm didn't have electricity, the cooler was typically chilled with ice that had been cut during the winter and stored in straw or sawdust.

Originally, farmers delivered the milk cans to the creamery themselves, said Don George, a former head of the state's dairy division, in a 1988 interview. One of the benefits of this system, George said, was that "this was the way the farmer communicated with all of his neighboring farmers.…There was a lot of chitchat that went on about dairy farming and other things." But waiting their turn to unload their milk was time consuming. Despite the community cohesion that delivering milk to the creamery instilled, as farms got larger, farmers increasingly decided they couldn't afford the time. They hired others to deliver the milk. Later, George said, creameries began picking up milk cans from the farms.

By 1955, many Vermont farmers were transitioning to the new bulk tanks, but the University of Vermont's Agricultural Experiment Station was skeptical that farmers would see much benefit. In a booklet titled "Economic Effects of Bulk Milk Handling in Vermont," agricultural economist Robert Sinclair examined the pros and cons of bulk tanks. Sinclair found that the tanks reduced some strenuous labor on the farm, mostly from farmers not having to lift milk cans (which weighed roughly ninety pounds when full) into coolers. He found, however, that farmers would save little or no time. The bulk tanks just required them to perform different tasks.

Sinclair questioned the claim by handlers that bulk tanks led to higher-quality milk, one of their main selling points. He said the tanks did a good job of rapidly cooling the milk, an important factor in milk quality, but stated that farmers could get similar results if they used new, seamless, stainless steel cans.

The biggest issue, from the farmers' perspective, was that bulk tanks were expensive. Installing a tank was a major investment, particularly for small farms. In an interview in the 1980s, Everett Willard, a former dairy farmer and master of the state Grange, said that installing a bulk tank could cost the equivalent of the net annual income for some farms. Part of that cost was often the expense of building a larger milk house to accommodate the bulk tank.

Handlers' costs of hauling milk from bulk tanks varied widely, Sinclair noted. It depended on the distance of the farm from the creamery and how many farms could be served on the same route. Large farms on main roads were the cheapest to service. Of course, thousands of Vermont farms were neither large nor on main roads, but the haulers' policies would change that.

A stainless steel bulk milk tank was a major investment for small farms. *Vermont State Archives.*

At first, handlers offered premiums for milk from farmers who switched to bulk tanks. Handlers then began refusing to accept milk stored in cans, so farmers who resisted buying bulk tanks had to switch to other handlers willing to take their milk. Eventually, those farmers ran out of options as more handlers began requiring bulk tanks.

Farms in remote parts of the state had no choice but to close. "I think the more modern times have put some farms out of business simply because of their location," said George. "If they're not convenient, some milk handlers just won't go and pick them up."

As small family farms closed, some sold their land to people who had recently moved to the state and to second-home owners. Others sold their land to the remaining farmers, who found they had to expand and increasingly mechanize their operations to satisfy a fluid milk market that demanded cheap milk. Farmers increased their herd sizes to reduce their per-gallon cost of producing milk. Larger herds forced farmers to switch from growing cash crops, such as oats and wheat, to hay, corn and silage crops to feed their many animals. To maximize yields, farmers turned to chemical fertilizers and hybrid seeds. To manage their expanded farm, farmers stopped tilling fields with horses and oxen and started using tractors.

New agricultural technologies have enabled the fewer than 1,000 dairy farms that remain to produce more milk together than did the 10,637 farms that existed in 1953. But they haven't left much room for the small, family dairy farms that once shaped Vermont society.

34

BEAUTY OVER BILLBOARDS

When Ted Riehle joined the Vermont legislature in the mid-1960s, he had a big idea. He wanted to rid the state of what he considered a blight on the landscape: the hundreds of billboards that lined the state's roadsides. It was an ambitious undertaking, particularly for a freshman lawmaker; perhaps Riehle was new enough to politics that he didn't realize the challenges ahead. The Vermont environmental movement owes a debt to Riehle for taking on this fight.

The debate over billboards wasn't exactly new. During the early decades of the twentieth century, American culture became increasingly car-centric. Responding to Americans' new mobility, businesses hit upon roadside advertisements as a way to connect with potential customers, particularly tourists. Writer Vrest Orton railed against the negative effects of Vermont's tourism boom, taking aim at "national advertisers, who have an urge to plaster all the roads retaining the least vestige of adjacent beauty with massive, gaudy and hideous sign-boards, so that it might truly be said, 'Behind the signboard lies Vermont.'"

By 1936, roughly 750 full-sized billboards and thousands of smaller advertising signs lined the state's roadsides. Of those billboards, 7 were located in Springfield and drew the ire of a group of residents who fought to have them removed. Using petitions, posters, handbills and threats of boycotts against advertisers, the group managed to have the billboards taken down. The Springfield drive grew into a statewide effort known as the Vermont Association for Billboard Restriction.

Billboards were once a common sight along Vermont roads. *Vermont State Archives.*

The number of billboards in Vermont only grew, however. But so, too, did opposition to them. The Rotary Club, the Grange and the Daughters of the American Revolution—some of the most influential social institutions of the era—protested what they saw as a commercial infringement on the public's right to view the landscape. They also argued that billboards were dangerous distractions for drivers.

Renowned journalist Dorothy Thompson, a part-time resident of Barnard, summarized the anti-billboard arguments in a letter to the *Rutland Herald* in 1937: "If aesthetic considerations do not move us, let us consider the matter from the standpoint of cold cash. Vermont has beauty to sell. Thousands and thousands of tourists come here every summer, for no other reason than that Vermont is lovely. They can see billboards from Connecticut to California. The absence of them is a positive asset."

The debate over billboards quickly became a matter of natives versus out-of-staters, according to scholar Blake Harrison in his 2006 book *The View from Vermont: Tourism and the Making of an American Rural Landscape.* Opponents called out-of-state billboard companies "parasites," arguing that they were destroying the beauty of the state for their own profit. And Vermont businesses that advertised on the signs were also putting their financial interests before the interests of the state. Vermont must be left "unspoiled," billboard opponents argued. Doing so made economic sense, they said, since tourists visited the state to see its beauty, not its billboards.

Billboard supporters, mainly advertisers and billboard companies, noted that opponents also relied on out-of-state support, in this case coming from tourists and part-time residents like Dorothy Thompson. Weren't billboard opponents putting the interests of people who could afford to travel above the interests of Vermont businesspeople trying to make a living? Besides, billboards sometimes provided tourists with useful information, they argued. Without the signs, tourists wouldn't be able to find their destinations.

The Vermont State Chamber of Commerce found itself stuck between competing business interests, but it ended up opposing billboards. Tourism in Vermont was unmistakably on the rise in the 1930s, and the chamber took the position that removing the billboards would benefit the state's economy, its residents and its visitors.

The state legislature tried to find a compromise. Representative Horace Brown of Springfield successfully championed a bill in 1939 that, while keeping billboards legal, limited their size and location. The closer to the road a sign was, the smaller it had to be. The law was challenged in court, but the Vermont Supreme Court found that property owners had no inherent right to place signs on land adjacent to public roadways. After the law's passage, the number of roadside signs fell roughly 50 percent between 1938 and 1943, but hundreds of billboards still graced the state's roadsides. Legislative efforts to curb billboards continued through the 1940s, '50 and '60s, but to no effect—until Ted Riehle took up the issue.

Riehle, a Republican representing South Burlington, told state senator Jim Jeffords that he planned to introduce a bill banning billboards. Jeffords said that if Riehle could get the bill through the Vermont House of Representatives, he would try to get it through the senate.

Riehle rallied support the old-fashioned way. This being an era when politicians and the press socialized freely, Riehle hosted parties at his Montpelier apartment for fellow legislators and journalists, and he may have won some over at these gatherings.

The billboard industry fought the proposed ban, hiring lobbyists to make their case. But the press dragged the lobbyists—and, by implication, their legislative friends—out of the comfortable, dark recesses of the statehouse and made them fair game for front-page exposure.

Billboard opponents found light-hearted ways to make their case. They popularized a poem riffing on a famous bit of verse by Ogden Nash:

> *I think I shall never see,*
> *A billboard as lovely as a tree.*
> *Perhaps unless the billboards fall,*
> *I shall never see a tree at all.*

A group gathers to watch the demolition of a billboard after the state legislature passed a bill banning them in 1968. *Vermont State Archives*.

The issue remained hot during the 1968 session. Billboard companies and advertisers labeled efforts to ban the signs "communist." Who was going to compensate them for removing the signs and giving up this inexpensive means of advertising? And what about all the lost and confused tourists if there were no signs to direct them to their accommodations and various attractions? Riehle and other billboard opponents suggested a compromise. The bill would phase out off-premises billboards over the next five years and would strictly regulate the size, location and lighting of on-premises signs, but the state would pay to post more discreet signs for local businesses.

The bill passed both chambers with strong Republican support and was signed by Governor Phil Hoff, though many of his fellow Democrats failed to support the legislation. Over the next five years, billboards disappeared and Vermont began to look once again much as it had in the days before the car.

For the next decade, the legislature passed a series of laws aimed at preserving Vermont's environment; they dealt with a serious litter problem with the bottle bill; addressed rampant and ill-conceived building projects with a development review law; and dealt with polluted rivers and streams with tighter regulations. Riehle and other advocates of the billboard law had successfully made the case that scenic beauty is essential to Vermont's identity and its economy.

BIBLIOGRAPHY

Books

Albers, Jan. *Hands on the Land: A History of the Vermont Landscape*. Cambridge, MA: MIT, 2002.

Alexander, Wayne H. *Runaway Pond, the Complete Story: A Compilation of Resources*. Glover, VT: Glover Historical Society, 2001.

Altherr, Thomas L. "'Will's Panther Club': Reverend William Ballou, the Irrepressible and Uncompromising Order of Pantherites, and the Chester, Vermont, Catamount-Sighting Controversy, 1934–1935." *Vermont History* (Winter/Spring 1998).

Bassett, T.D. Seymour. "The Cold Summer of 1816 in Vermont: Fact and Folklore." *New England Galaxy* (Summer 1973).

———. "The 1870 Campaign for Woman Suffrage in Vermont." *Vermont Quarterly* (1946).

Belanus, Betty Jane. *They Lit Their Cigars with Five Dollar Bills: The History of the Merino Sheep Industry in Addison County*. Middlebury, VT: National Endowment for the Humanities, 1977.

Benton, C., and S.F. Barry. *A Statistical View of the Number of Sheep in the Several Towns and Counties in Maine, New Hampshire, Vermont, Massachusetts, Rhode Island, Connecticut, New York, Pennsylvania, and Ohio: A Partial Account of the Number of Sheep in Virginia, Maryland, New Jersey, Delaware, and Kentucky in 1836: And an Account of the Principal Woollen Manufactories in Said States*. Cambridge, MA: Folson, Wells, and Thurston, 1837.

Brown, Richard D. "Lemuel Haynes and the Boundaries of Racial Tolerance on the Yankee Frontier, 1770–1820." *The New England Quarterly* (December 1988).

Citro, Joseph A. *Green Mountain Ghosts, Ghouls & Unsolved Mysteries*. Montpelier: Vermont Life, 1994.

Clifford, Deborah P. "The Drive for Women's Municipal Suffrage in Vermont: 1883–1917." *Vermont History* (Summer 1979).

———. "An Invasion of Strong-Minded Women: The Newspapers and the Woman Suffrage Campaign in Vermont in 1870." *Vermont History* (Winter 1975).

———. "The Women's War Against Rum." *Vermont History* (Summer 1984).

Cuneo, John R. *Robert Rogers of the Rangers*. New York: Richardson & Steirman, 1987.

Cutts, Mary Pepperell Sparhawk Jarvis. *The Life and Times of Hon. William Jarvis, of Weathersfield, Vermont*. New York: Hurd and Houghton, 1869.

Diane, Gilbert H. "The Birthplace of Chester A. Arthur." *Proceedings of the Vermont Historical Society* (March 1941).

Dickens, Charles, and T.P. James. *The Mystery of Edwin Drood Complete*. Brattleboro, VT: T.P. James, 1873.

Doyle, Arthur Conan. *The Alleged Posthumous Writings of Great Authors*. New York: Bookman, 1927.

Duffy, John J., and H. Nicholas Muller III. *Inventing Ethan Allen*. Hanover, NH: University of New England, 2014.

Falk, Candace, and Emma Goldman. *Made for America, 1890–1901*. Berkeley: University of California, 2003.

Fenn, Francis Talcott. *Merino Sheep in Vermont*. Hanover, NH: 1937.

Fischer, Dorothy Canfield. "Ann Story." *Vermont Quarterly* (1950).

Flanders, Ralph E. *Senator from Vermont*. Boston: Little, Brown, 1961.

Goldman, Emma. *Living My Life*. New York: Dover, 1970.

Graffagnino, J. Kevin. *The Shaping of Vermont: From the Wilderness to the Centennial, 1749–1877*. Rutland: Vermont Heritage, 1983.

Hahn, Michael T. *Ann Story: Vermont's Heroine of Independence*. Shelburne, VT: New England, 1996.

Harrison, Blake. "The Technological Turn: Skiing and Change in Vermont, 1930–1970." *Vermont History* (Summer/Fall 2003).

Hemenway, Abby Maria. *The Vermont Historical Gazetteer*. Burlington, VT: A.M. Hemenway, 1867–82.

Hill, Ellen C., and Marilyn S. Blackwell. *Across the Onion: A History of East Montpelier, Vermont, 1781 to 1981*. East Montpelier, VT: East Montpelier Historical Society, 1988.

Holmes, David R. *Stalking the Academic Communist: Intellectual Freedom and the Firing of Alex Novikoff*. London: Published for University of Vermont by University Press of New England, 1989.

Howe, George F. *Chester A. Arthur: A Quarter-Century of Machine Politics*. New York: F. Ungar, 1957.

Howrigan, Anne Rowley, Eleanor Wheeler Ballway and Joaquin P. Aja. *Fairfield, Vermont Reminiscences: 1763–1977*. Fairfield, VT: Fairfield Bicentennial Committee, 1977.

Jacobus, Melancthon W. "A Canal Across Vermont." *Vermont History* (1955).

Krull, Andrew S. "Dickens's Ghost Made the Improbable Choice." *Vermont Life* (Spring 1969).

Lane, Karen. "Old Labor Hall, Barre, Vermont: Preserving a Working Class Icon." *Labor's Heritage* (Spring/Summer 1999).

Loescher, Burt Garfield. *The History of Rogers' Rangers*. Bowie, MD: Heritage, 2001.

Ludlum, David M. *The Vermont Weather Book*. Montpelier: Vermont Historical Society, 1985.

Maurer, Carol. "A More Perfect Union Hall: In Barre, Vt., Local Workers Help Restore a Meeting Place That Witnessed the Labor Movement's Volatile Past." *Preservation* (September–October 2001).

Mazuzan, George T. "'Skiing Is Not Merely a Schport': The Development of Mount Mansfield as a Winter Recreation Area, 1930–1955." *Vermont History* (Winter 1972).

Meeks, Harold. "Stagnant, Smelly and Successful: Vermont's Mineral Springs." *Vermont History* (Winter 1979).

Melish, Joanne Pope. *Disowning Slavery: Gradual Emancipation and "Race" in New England, 1780–1860*. Ithaca, NY: Cornell University Press, 2000.

Millier, Brett C. "New York Summers in Vermont: The Round Table at Neshobe." *Historic Roots: A Magazine of Vermont History* (August 1998).

Nearing, Helen, and Scott Nearing. *The Good Life: How to Live Sanely and Simply in a Troubled World*. New York: Schocken, 1970.

Newkirk, McDonald. *Sleeping Lucy*. Chicago: M. Newkirk, 1973.

Olcott, Henry Steel, Alfred Kappes, T.W. Williams and Terence Barrow. *People from the Other World*. Rutland, VT: Charles E. Tuttle, 1972.

Reeves, Thomas C. *Gentleman Boss: The Life and Times of Chester Alan Arthur*. Newtown, CT: American Political Biography, 2002.

Rogers, Robert, and Timothy J. Todish. *The Annotated and Illustrated Journals of Major Robert Rogers*. Fleischmanns, NY: Purple Mountain, 2002.

Saillant, John. "Lemuel Haynes's Black Republicanism and the American Republican Tradition, 1775–1820." *Journal of the Early Republic* (Fall 1994).

Senghas, Reverend Robert E. "Joshua Young: Burlington Abolitionist." Sermon. First Unitarian Universalist Society, Burlington, Vermont, December 6, 1981.

Sherman, Michael. *Vermont State Government Since 1965*. Burlington: University of Vermont, 1999.

Sherman, Michael, Gene Sessions and P. Jeffrey Potash. *Freedom and Unity: A History of Vermont*. Barre: Vermont Historical Society, 2004.

Stevens, Jay. "When the Spirit World Touched Chittenden." *Yankee Magazine* (January 1987).

Stoat, Caroline Fuller. "The Center of Local Commerce: The Asa Knight Store of Dummerston, Vermont, 1827–1851." *Vermont History* (1985).

Storrs, Lee W. *The Green Mountains of Vermont*. New York: Holt, 1955.

Streeter, C.S. "Turkey Drives." *Vermont Quarterly* (1953).

Swift, Esther M. *Vermont Place-Names: Footprints of History*. Camden, ME: Picton, 1996.

Terkel, Studs. *American Dreams: Lost and Found*. New York: New Press, 1980.

Thompson, Zadock. *History of Vermont: Natural, Civil and Statistical in Three Parts, with an Appendix, 1853*. Burlington, VT: Thompson, 1853.

Truesdell, John W. *The Bottom Facts Concerning the Science of Spiritualism: Derived from Careful Investigations Covering a Period of 25 Years*. New York: Carleton, 1883.

Tuttle, Charles E., Jr. "Vermont and the Slavery Question." *Proceedings of the Vermont Historical Society* (1938).

Twynham, Leonard. "A Martyr for John Brown." *Opportunity: Journal of Negro Life* (September 1938).

Whorton, James C. *Nature Cures: The History of Alternative Medicine in America*. New York: Oxford University Press, 2004.

Wilson, Charles Morrow. *The Great Turkey Drive*. New York: McKay, 1964.

Young, Joshua. *The Funeral of John Brown*. Boston: New England Magazine, 1904.

Newspapers

Argus and Patriot (Montpelier, VT)
Bennington Banner
Boston Evening Transcript
Brattleboro Phoenix
Brattleboro Reformer
Burlington Free Press
Burlington Sentinel
Green Mountain Freeman (Montpelier, VT)
New Hampshire Sentinel (Keene, NH)
Middlebury Register
Rutland Herald
St. Albans Messenger
Vermont Chronicle (Windsor, VT)
Vermont Journal (Windsor, VT)

About the Author

M ark Bushnell worked for a dozen years as an editor for Vermont newspapers. Realizing that writers have more fun than editors, he began freelancing. Since 2002, he has written regularly about Vermont history, first for the *Rutland Herald* and *Barre-Montpelier Times Argus* and more recently a weekly column for VTDigger, a statewide news website. He is the author of *Discover Vermont! The Vermont Life Guide to Exploring Our Rural Landscape* and *It Happened in Vermont: From the French and Indian War to the Exposure of Maple Corner, Thirty-Two Events That Shaped the Green Mountain State.* He also contributed chapters to *Howard Dean: A Citizen's Guide to the Man Who Would Be President* and *Lake Champlain: An Illustrated History.* He lives in central Vermont with his wife, Susan Clark, and son, Harrison.

Visit us at
www.historypress.net